# Critical Conversations as Leadership

## Driving Change with Card Talk

## William Donohue, Ph.D.

Front Edge Publishing

Cover art and design by
Rick Nease
www.RickNeaseArt.com

Illustrations by Brandon James and Brad Schreiber
By Design Graphic Arts

Published by Front Edge Publishing
42015 Ford Rd., Suite 234
Canton, Michigan, USA

Front Edge Publishing specializes in speed and flexibility in
adapting and updating our books. We can include links to
video and other online media. We offer discounts on bulk purchases for special events, corporate training, and small groups.
We are able to customize bulk orders by adding corporate or
event logos on the cover and we can include additional pages
inside describing your event or corporation. For more information about our fast and flexible publishing or permission to use
our materials, please contact Front Edge Publishing at info@
FrontEdgePublishing.com.

# Contents

# Introduction

Leaders drive change. They had better not just react to change; they had better drive it.

That driving process happens through a series of critical conversations. Vision conversations with managers, performance appraisals with employees and sales negotiations with clients are all critical conversations. These are high-stakes exchanges. And, yes, we really can't lead without embracing these critical conversations and executing them well.

What is the best strategy for communicating? We all do it, but few of us think strategically about crafting a message for a specific audience in a critical situation. Instead of thinking strategically, many people default to their standard approach, which more often than not does not yield effective results. The approach we take in this book is called Card Talk.

The idea is that communication is really just a card game. When we talk, write a note, make a call or tap out a text, we play a card that reflects the role we're playing at that moment. A leader might play the Colleague Card with an employee in sharing technical data; alternatively, she could play the Visionary Card in a strategic planning meeting with her team when discussing business changes to meet client needs. Depending on your goal, you select the card that will work best to get your point across. From that card, you select a certain topic and then surround that topic with a style or tone that helps get your point across. This is the talk card we show in the critical conversation.

The specific purpose of the critical conversation becomes the card game we're playing. Effective communication is about selecting the right card—or cards— for the games being played, so that everyone can accomplish their communication goals. This book walks you through that process with many examples and exercises, so that you can think more strategically about how you get your point across.

# Card Talk and Card Games

## Chapter 1: The Card Talk Approach to Critical Conversations

Card Talk is about thinking strategically, or thinking ahead and not thinking (with your) behind. Why do so many of your verbal exchanges fail? Examples will be provided from various dialogues, including male/female; manager/employee; parent/child; and sales agent/customer.

## Chapter 2: Talk Games

Card games are your system for "communicating ahead" (thinking strategically) and not "communicating behind" (simply reacting). This chapter introduces talk cards, topics, styles, reciprocity, card hands, card decks and related terms. The key to successful business (and interpersonal) communication is to select the right talk cards in the right situation to win the game you want to play. But you can't do it unless you think strategically about what you're trying to do with your message.

## Chapter 3: Simple Steps for Playing Critical Conversation Games

There are four simple steps for winning critical conversation games: Name the game, have simple goals, select the right cards and play to win. How do these steps work, in relation to your communication style?

## Chapter 4: The Leader Card

The Leader Card is fundamental to playing and winning critical conversation games. This chapter defines the broad areas of the Leader Card and how it should be played.

# Critical Conversation Games Leaders Need to Win

## Chapter 5: The Casual Conversation Game

Sometimes we select a talk card that isn't the right one. What causes us to rely on one card? Our relationship with the other communicator may restrict our talk card choices. Our social identities might also limit our personal and professional decks of talk cards. In general, business professionals need a large deck of both personal and professional cards to give them the flexibility they need to play games effectively.

## Chapter 6: The Decision-making Game

As we know from Chapter 4, part of the Leader Card must include challenging the process, which means making better decisions. What do we know about how to make better decisions? What cards are essential in playing this game effectively? Where do most leaders fail when trying to win this game?

## Chapter 7: The Driving-change Game

Leaders engage in many critical conversations, almost on a daily basis. One of the more difficult conversations involves making changes in a policy or practice that is important for the organization. The key is knowing that driving change is a process: It requires multiple conversations and multiple talk cards. What do these conversations consist of and how can this game be constructive?

## Chapter 8: The Negotiation Game

Negotiating effectively requires building value. What does it mean to build value in resolving differences? What is conflict—and which cards, topics and styles typically emerge in conflict? The problem that most leaders have is assuming that the Negotiation Game is adversarial. It is not. Building value means that negotiation is a collaborative game that requires collaborative tactics.

## Chapter 9: The Performance Appraisal Game

Leaders know how to manage talent. They have a clear understanding of what performance is required to be effective, and they hold people accountable for that performance. But the separator is that effective leaders know how to inspire and energize team members, to get the most out of each: They know how to have the critical conversation about performance that is constructive.

## Chapter 10: The Presenting Game

Effective leaders can get up in front of the team and present ideas clearly and convincingly. The classic mistake new leaders make in giving presentations is playing only one card. Multiple cards, along with the right combination of digital and personal media, are needed to reach audiences. What do effective presentations look like?

## Chapter 11: The Vision Game

Perhaps the most important expectation that followers have of leaders is that they lay out a vision for the organization. The first and second most important questions a leader must answer are, "Where are we going?" and "Why are we going there?" Leaders must provide simple answers to these two questions to capture the attention of followers. This chapter talks about what a vision is and how to play the Vision Game, or the communication effort needed to sell and sustain this vision.

### Chapter 12: The Customer Engagement Game

Customers' relationships with companies have changed. Customers want to engage with companies and build their brand. Playing that game successfully requires a wide range of personal and professional cards so customers feel welcomed and that their input is valued.

# Playing Tips

### Chapter 13: Avoiding Common Mistakes

What are some common tactical mistakes in playing a hand? Common communication mistakes include:

1. Overplaying one card
2. Playing the wrong topic for the situation
3. Playing the wrong style for the person or situation at hand
4. Not recognizing the card(s) you're being asked to play

This chapter will present examples of these situations, which are common missteps in business communication that may limit your professional success.

# The Card Talk Approach to Critical Conversations

I had started the communication seminar the way I usually do: Asking the audience of high-performing executives to name the most pressing concern at their businesses. Eight or nine hands went up in the air.

One of them belonged to Chad, a 40-something business CEO from the southern United States who had grown up in the family enterprise. His father retired at 65, leaving Chad the leader of a multi-million-dollar company, a team of devoted employees and a bucketful of new challenges.

Chad expressed frustration at being unable to build consensus for change across the company. He wanted to invest in more automated food processing equipment; he felt that the human resources processes, including recruiting, were antiquated. Chad thought that the software was outdated, and that even the phone system was not serving the business well.

But whenever he broached these topics with his team—all long-term employees, most of them family friends and friends of one another, after all these years—every significant change was resisted.

"We're doing just fine."

"Why spend the money?"

"It would be too disruptive."

And the employees had a host of other reasons to keep things mostly as they were.

The new CEO, who had a broader view of the industry, didn't think his company was doing "just fine." Chad knew he needed to drive change in order to remain at the leading edge of the industry, but time was drifting by and he was becoming increasingly frustrated.

"My people are stuck in the past and I can't get them to see the future—and the need for change," he said to me. "How can I press my case and make this happen? Do I need to fire them all?"

A light murmur went through the audience of executives. Chad wasn't the only one facing resistance from good employees, it seemed.

I asked Chad how he was presenting his case to the employees. He replied, "Well, I have been there a long time—everybody knows me, how hard I work and how I want the business to succeed for the next 20 to 30 years. I keep sharing my vision for the future, but it's like I'm speaking to the walls. And the company is too big for me to force changes—I'd lose the team.

"I guess they like the old ways of doing things, but that's not good for the business," Chad concluded dispiritedly.

This topic got the other leaders' attention, for sure.

I explained to the business leaders that we all know change is a common problem, and that in this case, it might be a classic Card Talk problem, as well. I gave a quick explanation of communication and strategically selecting the right talk cards in every business interaction. I discussed the importance of having many professional and personal cards, or card decks, that could be selected for any specific communication game or activity.

"Chad, you've communicated with your team mostly playing the Friend Card—maybe even the Son-of-the-Boss Card—for the last 20 years. When you were in that role, the topics were personal—possibly because of your father's shadow—and your

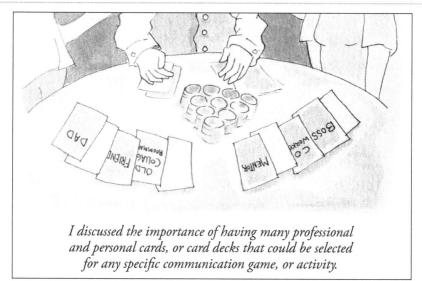

*I discussed the importance of having many professional
and personal cards, or card decks that could be selected
for any specific communication game, or activity.*

topics didn't challenge anyone. You weren't perceived as the
leader or top decision-maker in a mid-size family business.

"Now you want to—and you have to—play the Boss Card,
or Leader Card. On the Leader Card, the topics are business-fo-
cused and may be professionally confrontational," I said. "I
think your people aren't ready for you to play the Leader Card;
when you open your mouth to speak, they only expect the
Friend Card. And they want to play the Friend Card back at you.
As you say, it's what they know."

The good news is that it's possible for Chad and anyone else
to change company dynamics through communication. You can
reset the team culture to follow new leadership, whether in a
family-run company or a large corporation.

I suggested a retreat with the leadership team as a way for
Chad to establish his own use of the Leader Card. Chad needed
to get away from the business setting for a few days and let
everyone get to know him as the boss, so that they could listen
to his new ideas in that context.

Chad needed to declare it a new day at his father's former
company with a significant departure from business-as-usual.
Then he had to be prepared to play the Leader Card, with a
significantly smaller focus on the Friend Card and no Son-of-
the-Boss Card.

# Transforming from Buddy to Boss

If you've been promoted from within or work in a family-run business, you may need to strategically consider how to develop the Leader Card through communication. Here are a few tips:

- **Borrow power.** If there's a layer of leadership above you, work with your supervisor to find situations in which he or she can publicly reinforce your role. Show people that you have the Leader Card.

- **Break with tradition.** In a family-run business, breaking even a couple of less-important traditions can signal a new leader at the helm. Maybe it's as simple as repainting the lunchroom or revising the logo.

- **Retract the Friend Card a little bit.** Adopt a more businesslike approach in meetings and engage in less office chitchat. Be friendly, but do not let this be the dominant talk card when trying to transform your role.

- **Build your deck of business cards.** Leaders are expected to be experts. Pick an area in which you're particularly knowledgeable and look for settings in which you can share your thoughts about those topics without being overbearing. Develop a few key cards, such as the Expert Card, the Facilitator Card and the Conflict Manager Card.

- **Play more leadership games.** Don't hide from leadership opportunities; look for them. The more practice you get playing the Leader Card, the better.

I'll give more tips on developing the Leader Card later. But for now, let's continue to tease out the idea that we are playing a hand of cards every time we communicate.

We obviously can't double-think everything we say when we open our mouths. But when we see challenging situations and important business deals on the horizon, we need to pull back briefly and think about our talk card playing strategy.

# What are Talk Cards?

Here's the reality: The most common communication mistake we make in business is playing the wrong talk card at the wrong time. We may have all the skills we need to be successful in business, but rethinking how we play our hand of talk cards can revolutionize the success of our interpersonal and leadership interactions.

I recently coached Kelly, a rather soft-spoken woman, on an important project. Kelly had been selected by upper management in her company for a leadership position. Yet while she had great technical expertise and was a very fast learner, her communication skills and lack of professional demeanor were viewed as a barrier in being effective in a leadership position. Kelly didn't talk or look the part.

First, I asked Kelly to reflect on her appearance. I asked her if she believed she looked like other leaders in the organization. After some reflection, Kelly offered that her appearance was more consistent with the culture of her unit, which was very informal. She was quickly able to provide some strategies for looking more the part, particularly since she was going to have to travel in more upscale, professional circles.

Next we focused on her verbal communication. Kelly's reserved approach, combined with various verbal hedges (she always ended her sentences with "Right?"), communicated uncertainty. Yet she didn't really see it at first. When I recorded her giving a presentation, she heard it immediately and couldn't believe she sounded so weak. After that rude awakening, she quickly altered her choices and began speaking more forcefully and less tentatively. Combined with her more professional appearance, Kelly now rocks as a leader.

That's what communication really is. When we talk, write a note, make a call or tap out a text, we play cards. We select a certain topic and then surround that topic with a style or tone that helps get our point across. This **package** is the **talk card** we show to the other person.

Whenever we communicate, we have three distinct goals. First, we reveal the **purpose** of our message: to inform, persuade, tease, scold, etc. Second, we want to establish a specific type of **relationship** between the communicators, and we show our talk cards to do that. For example, Chad wanted to be seen as the boss, so he had to learn to play the Boss Card. Third, we seek to establish our **identity,** or image, as a competent, attractive and interesting person who can't be pushed around.

Every message contains all three pieces of information about our goals, and each is important in getting our point across. For now, let's focus on talk cards, because it's a useful way for thinking about how all three goals work together to communicate ideas.

# Balancing Talk Cards

Marvin was a coaching client. He was the CEO of a mid-size information technology service firm that was growing rapidly but experiencing costly errors.

Marvin had difficulty getting his team to open up in meetings. He knew that he needed their help to solve problems and was stumped as to why his management team thought he was cold and uncaring. After observing Marvin in informal settings with his team throughout the day, I thought I had the answer. Marvin could not play the Friend Card.

When friends reveal personal information about themselves and family members, they make themselves a little bit vulnerable and a little bit more human. Friends ask others about their personal activities. They build bonds with one another.

To quote the old maxim by John C. Maxwell, noted American author, speaker and pastor: "People don't care how much you know until they know how much you care."

Marvin never showed that he cared. He always played the CEO Card like he was running a marathon board meeting. There were no personal topics that humanized Marvin to the

*After observing Marvin in informal settings with his team throughout the day, I thought I had the answer. Marvin could not play a Friend Card.*

group. As a result, Marvin's team really didn't trust him and generally would not open up to him.

I then told Marvin about the Card Talk concept. I indicated that a card is your whole communication package, which includes both **topic** and **style** elements.

The content is the idea, or *topic*, that people expect to see when a card is played. For example, when people are having a drink after work, they expect to see the Friend Card come out and to hear interesting personal information and stories. The *style* part deals with how friendly, how formally and how powerfully the topics are presented. Style gives emphasis to the topic. Style fills in meaning behind the idea. Style and topic work together in the message package.

When playing the Friend Card, the topics are discussed in a very friendly and informal manner, and in a style that does not indicate power in the relationship. People are showing the Friend Card when they kick back and talk about their families, sports, politics or other things friends usually discuss.

As a result of this discussion, Marvin asked me to play an informal chitchat game with him so that he could practice using the Friend Card. Of course, he was fully capable of playing the Friend Card, because he had a loving family and good friends.

Marvin had the mistaken idea that a successful CEO should never show the Friend Card at work. Not true! In fact, the higher up the ladder you climb, the more you'll be expected to play talk cards with differing styles as you interact with more people. Relationships are the name of the game if you have people working for you—and if you expect people to network with you.

When I last spoke with Marvin, the climate in his company had improved significantly. Employees believed he had "loosened up," and they were more willing to open up to him in business and in casual conversations, which was leading to significant improvement in the business itself.

Marvin's situation illustrates how many of us fail, at times, to think through our communication choices. Rather than strategizing at key times, we tend to go with our default behaviors—what we do most often or what we are most comfortable doing in a particular setting. This is called **trained incapacity**, and it can be a problem as work and life responsibilities become more complex. In trained incapacity, we become so practiced at talking one way in a certain situation that we can't change even when the situation demands a shift.

This trained incapacity problem became painfully apparent to a star salesman, Philip (who attended one of my workshops). He was a good contributor in the session, as one would expect from a star performer.

Near the end of the workshop, Philip asked my advice on a personal problem. Philip said that he and his teenage daughter were having trouble getting along and communicating with each another. Rather than giving him advice about this problem, I asked him to describe how he communicates at work.

"I have a very stressful job. I'm on the road all day, seeing many clients, and when I return to the office at 4:30 every afternoon, I have to return 20 phone calls before the day is done and everyone leaves their offices," he said. "I have to solve every client's problem in minutes!"

I responded, "Wow, that's a high-pressure job! Now, let me see if I can tell you how your interactions with your daughter typically go. She comes to you and begins talking about a specific problem, and you quickly interrupt her and tell her exactly what to do. Then she gets mad at you and doesn't at all appreciate your insights, and she stomps out of the room. Is that about it?"

"Yes," he said. "How did you know?"

I responded, "Philip, you're using the Salesperson Card to talk with your daughter instead of using the Parent Card. Your daughter is not a client. As an almost-grown teenager, she's still a daughter—and that requires the Parent Card.

"Playing the Parent Card to give personal advice should be friendly, informal and low-power. It requires listening and not interrupting. Maybe a high-power style works with clients in a hurry, but it doesn't work with teenage daughters," I chuckled.

Marvin couldn't change from the Boss Card to the Friend Card. Philip didn't recognize that he needed to shift from the very successful Salesperson Card to the Parent Card when the situation called for it. They both suffered from trained incapacity. But by becoming more thoughtful about their talk card choices, each of them was able to communicate more effectively and improve personal and business situations.

## Talk Card Self-Assessment Inventory

When I tell people these stories, the first thing that pops into their head is: "Gee, I wonder if I'm playing the right cards at the right time to get my point across?" Well, let's see! Take a look at these questions and answer "yes," "no" or "maybe." Then tally your results at the end of the quiz.

| Talk Card Self-Assessment | Yes | No | Maybe |
|---|---|---|---|
| 1. I can play the **Friend Card** with my boss at least sometimes. | | | |

| Talk Card Self-Assessment | Yes | No | Maybe |
|---|---|---|---|
| 2. I feel free to play the **Friend Card** with my co-workers anytime I like. | | | |
| 3. I can play the **Leader Card** at work when needed. | | | |
| 4. I have no trouble switching from the **Friend Card** to a **Leader Card** when needed. | | | |
| 5. I like playing the **Colleague Card** at work to promote teamwork. | | | |
| 6. People expect me to play the **Expert Card** when discussing a problem. | | | |
| 7. I enjoy playing the **Salesperson Card** when I have an idea or concept to sell. | | | |
| 8. I know how to play the **Boyfriend/Girlfriend Card** or **Husband/Wife Card** when discussing difficult personal subjects. | | | |
| 9. My friends would say I can play the **Comedian Card** to break up a boring situation. | | | |

| Talk Card Self-Assessment | Yes | No | Maybe |
|---|---|---|---|
| 10. I can easily switch out of my work-related cards and play my personal cards when I'm home. | | | |
| 11. I have played a **Mentor or Coach Card** at some point in my life. | | | |
| 12. I am, or would be, good at playing a **Parent Card.** | | | |

If you checked "yes" to at least eight of the 12 questions, you are fairly comfortable with your Card Talk inventory. If you checked "yes" on fewer than eight, you may be relying on a very limited number of cards when you communicate. People who have experience playing 20 or 30 different talk cards can communicate more effectively across challenging business situations.

Also notice the range of cards mentioned in the quiz. Let's look at each of these 10 key cards to better understand its goal.

## Ten Key Talk Cards:

1. **Friend Card:** Building personal relationships
2. **Leader Card:** Helping a group or organization accomplish its goals
3. **Colleague Card:** Sharing professional insights and information
4. **Expert Card:** Providing technical information to move a task forward
5. **Salesperson Card:** Selling an idea, concept, service or product
6. **Boyfriend/Girlfriend Card:** Strengthening bonds in an intimate relationship

7. **Husband/Wife Card:** Helping to manage family complexities

8. **Comedian Card:** Ingesting humor or something playful into a message

9. **Mentor/Coach Card:** Providing advice on personal or professional matters

10. **Parent Card:** Guiding a child's understanding and choices

Throughout this book I will ask you to reflect on your talk cards. These 10 cards will help you start thinking about the cards you have to work with when communicating with others.

# Developing New Talk Cards

Mostly, our cards are divided into two categories: **personal** and **professional**.

**Personal** cards are typically the ones we develop first within our families and communities. We use them most often when we communicate.

The Parent Card is a good example of a well-developed personal card in my deck, as I'm the dad of six boys. But I can't have just one card when interacting with my boys. I am also asked to play the Expert Card, the Comedian Card, the Christian Card and many others, in the course of our interactions. In fact, most conversations in just about every setting involve switching back and forth between personal and professional cards.

Think of your conversations at work. Someone will ask, "How are you?" and you might reply with the Friend Card, talking about your weekend with friends and family members, before you switch to the Colleague Card and start talking about business issues you're facing this week.

**Professional** or work-related cards include topics we're expected to be able to discuss on the job. For example, over the years I've studied hostage negotiations and worked with police to discover the best way to develop and play the Police

Negotiator Card. The first thing these crisis negotiators are taught is that some topics are available for discussion and others are not. Available topics include food, comfort, media exposure and other issues related to conditions inside the hostage area. Unavailable topics include things like transportation off the site.

A key in developing the professional Police Negotiator Card is being able to discuss personal topics using the Friend Card, in order to develop a relationship with the hostage-taker. Once the relationship is formed, then they can exchange information, explore issues and ultimately cut a deal to release the hostages.

That makes sense on paper, yet asking police negotiators to strategically play the Friend Card when communicating with hostage-takers may appear to run counter to their culture.

Years ago, the police officer was taught to communicate in a commanding fashion in order to quickly take control of a situation. An officer on a hostage negotiation team needs special training to learn how to strategically switch between the Friend Card and and the Officer Card in order to develop a relationship with the hostage taker and resolve the crisis.

This example illustrates that we rarely play a single card at a time. We often mix personal and professional cards.

My wife and I mix cards because she is my business partner. One minute we're talking about business topics, and then in the next, we'll switch to family matters. It happens all the time. Switching back and forth between personal and professional cards opens up a conversation and enables people to get to know one another.

The question is this: How do we mix and match our cards in different situations to be effective? Before we answer this question, let's drill down further into the concept of talk cards and how they work.

# How Do Talk Cards Work?

Card play is organized around three key principles:

1. **Cards assume goals.** Every card we play in every situation assumes a specific goal. The communicator wants to have a specific impact on others. People want to make the sale, deal with an employee complaint, console a friend or simply share the events of the day. Even if the communicator cannot clearly express his or her goal when forming a message, the receivers will assume the messages are goal-directed. People always think: "What is he getting at?" "Why is he bringing this up?" The key is to be thoughtful about the goal, or goals, and play the best set of cards for those goals.

2. **Cards are reciprocated.** When a card is shown, it specifically but indirectly asks the others to play its reciprocal card—the one that goes with it. Playing the Teacher Card asks the others to play the Student Card. Showing the Leader Card asks the listeners to play the Follower Card. The strategic question is whether the card you're asking the receiver to play is effective in accomplishing your goal. I don't want my students playing the Student Card for long periods of time because it's a very passive card—they just sit and stare. When I shift between several cards during a presentation, it asks the audience to switch to more active cards. This keeps them on their toes and tuned in to the presentation.

3. **Cards shape the context.** Playing the Comedian Card keeps the context light; playing the Friend Card keeps it personal. The Leader Card establishes a businesslike situation. If the listener reciprocates the card (e.g., laughs at the Comedian Card) the speaker can play it again when needed.

I pay a lot of attention to how leaders establish their credibility with various audiences. Based on these three principles, I advise executives to:

- **Be deliberate about card choices.** Have clear goals about which cards are likely to be most effective in specific situations. Be aware!

- **Keep several cards in your hand.** *Never* bore an audience with just one card all the time. Mix it up. Hold and play at least three cards in every situation. In professional situations it's OK to play a personal card briefly and share a family story, for example.

- **Mix up styles on cards.** Shake it up occasionally. Be friendly sometimes, and stern other times. Try a formal approach mixed up with informal words or comments. Take a direct approach at times, and be ambiguous at others. The key is diversity. Audiences will love it.

- **Look for Leader Card opportunities.** People expect leaders to be knowledgeable about important topics. Audiences value this knowledge, which gives you permission to play the Leader Card more frequently. Over time your leadership becomes the norm, rather than the exception.

Playing the Leader Card effectively requires giving timely, accurate information using a friendly but formal (no verbal slips or "umms") and moderately powerful style (speaking authoritatively). People respond well to this style mix. I asked Kelly to practice this approach many times. Her team responded well to the more powerful style. They remarked, "Kelly really knows her stuff."

There's little doubt that communicating strategically requires selecting the right mix of cards, topics that people want to know about and styles that enhance the significance of these topics.

This card play, over time, presents our identity—it tells others how we want to be seen and how we want them to think about us. This is an important point. It speaks to the issue of why we play talk cards in the first place, how we pick cards to play and how we work to win these card games. Let's focus first on this identity issue and why we play cards.

# Why Do We Play Talk Cards?

When we flash one card or another, what truly drives our card selection in any given situation? At the most basic level, we communicate in order to impact others in some way. We might want to tell a joke, alter an attitude or belief, or persuade someone to perform some behavior. The goal part of the message is generally what drives the topic, or concept, part of the card.

It's the concept that most people think about when communicating. They might want someone to pass the salt at the dinner table and focus more on getting the salt than on the style attached to the request.

Certainly we think about style when we see what style others are using to form their messages, particularly if their style is different than we expect.

Ron, an executive with a financial services firm, is an African-American, and is very adept at switching styles. Ron would play the Suburban Guy Card with me and the other executives with no hint of any accent different from my own. One day, when Ron and I were at lunch, a couple of his African-American friends stopped by the table to say hi. They greeted him with a more urban style of communication. Ron reciprocated with the African-American Urban Card while simultaneously playing the Friend Card. Ron's skill in card switching was remarkable.

We talked about it extensively. Ron said that displaying the African-American Urban Card was mandatory with that group of friends. His ability to maintain childhood friendships hinged on displaying that card in their presence. He recalled that they made this requirement clear and explicit. They knew that he played a professional card around me and his employees, but it was the wrong approach with them.

# Our Personal Identity and Face Needs

As it turns out, the style part of a card—and often the topic part, as well—is specifically selected to display our identity. Our identity is the set of beliefs we hold about who we are. You might believe you're smart and tough, but also caring and expressive. You might believe you're attractive and physically fit. The full range of beliefs about every aspect of your life constitutes your identity.

These beliefs about ourselves determine how we present ourselves to others. In other words, they determine what **face** or impression we present to the world. If you want to be seen as smart, tough and attractive, then you say and do things that present that **face** to the world. If I want to be seen as a competent leader, then I have to create that facethrough my language choices, actions and physical appearance.

In general, we can place our face, or our impression management needs, into two general categories: positive face and negative face.

**Positive face** is the desire to be seen as attractive, desirable, interesting and effective. It generally translates into the desire to be respected for who you are. Ron wanted to be respected by people from many different groups, as many of us do, so he changed his language and appearance to achieve positive face from his peers. Kelly needed to fit in with her team and be respected as its leader. Philip needed to gain respect from his daughter, as her parent. Do you have the cards that enable you to achieve positive face in any situation, so you can fit in?

**Negative face** is the desire not to be pushed around or controlled. People want freedom and choice. Violating someone's negative face would involve asking them—or even more severely, demanding them—to do something. We generally use politeness strategies to keep from severely violating someone's negative face, but sometimes we aren't successful and they get offended anyway.

Maybe you can relate to Janice, a woman working in a support position in a large company. She had worked in that support position for 15 years and had made many friends among her co-workers. Suddenly, she was promoted into a supervisory position in her unit. After years of playing the Friend Card with co-workers, she now had to create and play the Leader Card.

From a face-needs perspective, Janice wanted to support her positive face by being seen as a competent and effective supervisor. She also wanted to support her negative face needs by having the freedom to operate as an effective supervisor. So creating an effective Leader Card—or any card, for that matter—involves both being seen as competent in playing that card (positive face) and having the freedom to do the job as required (negative face).

Unfortunately, Janice never had the opportunity to create the Leader Card before taking the promotion. She was promoted because of her job knowledge, and not necessarily because of her communication flexibility. By promoting her without first training her on how to switch between the Friend Card and the Leader Card, the company was placing Janice at risk for failure.

How can we help people like Janice? The most difficult job transitions for people generally involve developing the talk cards they need to assume their new positions. Janice's supervisor could have helped her develop her use of the Leader Card by preparing her for the kinds of challenges she would face in her new role.

# Talk Games

I recently had lunch with Jim, a prominent hostage negotiator. Jim is a police detective who has worked many hostage incidents over several years. I asked him to recall one of his most memorable cases. He thought for a minute and said, "It's probably not what you think. Actually, most of what I do is suicide prevention."

Jim went on to recall that recently he was called to a scene in which a woman was standing on a girder of a very tall bridge, ready to jump. She had parked her car on the bridge, holding up rush-hour traffic, and then had gotten out of her car and climbed on a girder over the water, trying to summon the courage to jump. When Jim arrived on the scene, he saw the woman and slowly approached her.

These incidents are difficult for hostage negotiators because there are competing interests at work. On the one hand, Jim's primary goal is saving the woman's life. That goal is balanced by his opposing interest in resolving the issue quickly so that the bridge can be reopened to traffic. These competing interests require Jim to play very different cards: the Police Officer Card, to resolve the situation quickly, and the Negotiator Card, to secure the woman's safety.

*As Jim approached the woman, he knew that he had to hold more than just the Negotiator Card.*

As Jim approached the woman, he knew that he had to hold more than just the Negotiator Card. He may need to play the Friend Card, the Counselor Card and the Comedian Card, and perhaps one or two others as well. He came up to her slowly, knowing two things: one, that she was very distraught and wanted to kill herself to relieve the pain; and two, that in spite of her desperation, part of her wanted to live. Otherwise she would have already jumped.

Jim introduced himself, and the woman responded with her name. That was a good sign! Then she dumped her story. She had caught her husband cheating on her with a much younger woman, so she believed she had nothing to lose. Jim then played the Friend Card and asked questions about her family. She reported that she had two daughters, one 12 and the other 15. He then asked a lot of questions about the youngest daughter and her need for a mother. After several exchanges, the woman reconsidered and came off the bridge in tears.

The real value of this Card Talk idea is not just analyzing which cards we have and don't have; we must know which cards are in our deck so we can select the best cards to win the game.

So: What is a talk card game, what are game rules and what does it mean to "win"?

A talk card game is each person's definition of the task or activity that is driving the communication. As people communicate, they start playing the cards they have selected for that general occasion and immediately try to figure out what's happening. What are we doing here? Are we just talking? Or, are we trying to do something specific?

Upon arriving on the scene, the hostage negotiator quickly learned that he had to talk the woman off the bridge. His goal was to win the Suicide Prevention Game. As he approached the woman on the bridge, she began talking to him about her personal concerns, thereby playing the Self-disclosure Game. To win, the woman had to be understood and to achieve some emotional support for her crisis. The negotiator won by making sure the woman did not harm herself.

For Jim, the question was this: Which cards would be needed to connect with this woman so she could more rationally reflect on her plight? The official Police Officer Card might be too powerful and too formal to quickly build a relationship. Instead, Jim played the Counselor Card and asked lots of questions, provided some meaningful reflections and proposed some different ways of looking at the situation. The style choices were aimed at lowering power and showing an informal, personal touch in conversation while being friendly and engaging.

Playing the Counselor Card essentially asked the woman to play the Client Card. By opening up, the woman agreed to play the Client Card and reveal her story. That allowed the negotiator to help the woman reflect on her situation and think about her daughters, as opposed to focusing on the pain she was experiencing in her marriage.

Often, people begin communicating and are unsure what game they're playing. Flirting is played this way. What starts out as the Casual Conversation Game, played between interested parties, may turn into the Flirting Game, in which both parties switch to more personal topics using a very friendly, informal and low-power style. It's what makes flirting fun! The ambiguity adds interest and intrigue to the courtship dance.

Card games start with one person showing a specific card, the other person seeing the card, and then that person choosing a card to play in response. Let's say the person chooses to recipro-cate and play a complementary card, just like the woman did in response to the hostage negotiator. As this process evolves, peo-ple get a sense of what they're doing—they define the activity. This activity then becomes the game.

When Jim pulled out the Counselor Card in the first exchange, the troubled woman could have rejected that card if she didn't want to talk to the police negotiator. She could have either ignored the negotiator or responded defensively to the Police Officer Card that she might have imagined he was play-ing. The fact that the negotiator was able to quickly establish a rapport and exchange some very important information indi-cated that the woman accepted the Counselor Card and tacitly agreed to play the Client Card, and "receive" therapy.

In many circumstances, misreading cards—and, by extension, misreading proposed games—can have severe consequences. In divorce mediation, the mediator's goal is to help divorcing par-ties reach a custody, visitation or property division agreement. In broad terms, the mediator's job is to read each party's cards, figure out if they are playing the same game, and then decide if it's a productive game that will result in a "win," or an effective agreement.

I have conducted several analyses of actual divorce mediation transcripts. In many custody disputes, a judge might force par-ties into mediation to create a parenting plan for their children. In this circumstance, one or more of the parties might angrily play the Husband or Wife Card instead of playing the more cooperative Parent Card.

I have seen husbands verbally abuse wives in venting their fears and frustrations. Mediators are trained to acknowledge the Husband and Wife cards, but shift parties from the Marital Argument Game to the Parenting Plan Game. The Marital

Argument Game is often a tough one to terminate because it has a lot of energy, and the divorcing parties have it well-practiced. Turning that around requires a very deliberate and highly structured process to keep things moving along constructively.

Below is a list of 10 games that most professionals need to learn to play in the course of their professional lives. How many are you comfortable playing?

## Talk Card Games Inventory

| Talk Card Game Self-Assessment | Yes | No | Sometimes |
|---|---|---|---|
| 1. I enjoy playing the **Casual Conversation Game** with my employees. | | | |
| 2. I am confident in my ability to run an effective **Business Meeting Game.** | | | |
| 3. I am comfortable playing the **Mingling Game** with colleagues at professional events. | | | |
| 4. I have no trouble switching between personal and professional card games. | | | |
| 5. I do not avoid playing the **Conflict Resolution Game** when I need to step into a dispute. | | | |

| Talk Card Game Self-Assessment | Yes | No | Sometimes |
|---|---|---|---|
| 6. Playing the **Employee Evaluation Meeting Game** is something I do well. | | | |
| 7. I initiate conversations about new ideas on a regular basis through the **Innovation Game**. | | | |
| 8. I occasionally play the **Personal Advice Game** with colleagues when it's appropriate. | | | |
| 9. I like to play the **Joke Around Game** sometimes to keep the climate friendly in the office. | | | |
| 10. I am effective in giving precise instructions when playing the **Information-giving Game**. | | | |

If you checked "yes" to at least eight of the 10 questions, you are fairly comfortable with your ability to play talk card games. If you checked "yes" to fewer than eight, your game-playing confidence may be limited by the number of cards in your hand when you communicate. Notice the range of card games mentioned in the inventory. Let's look at each one to better understand its goal:

*Personal Advice Game: Helping to manage personal complexities.*

- **Casual Conversation Game:** Building personal relationships
- **Business Meeting Game:** Helping a group or organization accomplish its goals
- **Mingling Game:** Networking with colleagues and clients
- **Conflict Resolution Game:** Working through identity challenges
- **Employee Evaluation Meeting Game:** Creating professional development opportunities
- **Innovation Game:** Selling an idea, concept, service or product
- **Personal Advice Game:** Helping to manage personal complexities
- **Joke Around Game:** Making the climate warm and friendly
- **Information-giving Game:** Providing professional information in a clear and effective manner

The idea that whenever we talk we play talk games suggests winners and losers. Let's further explore what it means.

# "Winning" Talk Card Games

In talk card games, are there winners and losers? The short answer is: Absolutely. We all win and lose games frequently.

"Winning" a talk card game means that both participants accomplished their communication goals—the talk card play produced the desired results.

*Team members win the Business Meeting Game when they successfully move through their agenda.*

Parties in a divorce mediation win when they craft a parenting agreement. Team members win the Business Meeting Game when they successfully move through their agenda.

In the suicide attempt example, the police officer was successful in achieving his goal of talking the woman off the girder. The troubled woman also won in the sense that she was able to refocus her life on her children rather than focus only on her marital despair.

These examples point to the typical path of Card Talk success—that is, when both parties show the same card over several exchanges, indicating that they are playing the same game. They have achieved **synchrony** in the sense that they are on the same page.

Again, the card players may disagree substantively with one another. Maybe they are even fighting. But the key is that they are playing the same game, and whenever that happens, the chances for at least understanding to occur are very high.

I have seen the power of synchrony achieve success across several research projects:

- When husbands and wives play the same games in divorce mediation, they are much more likely to negotiate a parenting plan for their children.

- When physicians and patients synchronize their games, patients are much more likely to provide more extensive information that is useful for their treatment.

- When hostage negotiators synchronize with hostage-takers, the police are much more likely to achieve a negotiated ending to the crisis.

In other words, synchrony is essential in producing a win for both parties. Remember Philip, who had trouble talking with his daughter? He played the Salesperson Card, and she wanted the Parent Card. They could not synchronize.

The lesson here is that winning depends on achieving synchrony. Achieving synchrony requires:

- Reading one's own and others' cards correctly

- Determining if parties are playing the same game

- Knowing how to expand the rules of the game in order to enhance opportunities for synchrony

Now let's take a look at rules and how to play them.

# Game Rules

Every Card Talk game has two sets of rules for proper play: rules about what topics are appropriate, and rules about what styles are acceptable. Of course, the rules depend on how communicators define the game. Once that label is set, then the topic and style rules become clear. The critical point is that a clear understanding of the game is very important. You must know what game you're playing to have any chance of winning it.

For example, if the game has a formal definition, like an employee evaluation or performance appraisal, then the rules are clearer but also more constraining. In a rigid situation like this, a relatively few number of business topics are acceptable to discuss, while others are out-of-bounds. It would be appropriate to talk about skills required for a specific job, but improper to talk about the kind of deodorant people use or what their home lives are like.

Styles are also constrained. In casual conversation, use of bad grammar or mildly profane language signals a very informal situation. But in the Evaluation Employee Meeting Game, this level of informality is not appropriate. The supervisor might even say, "We don't use that kind of language here."

Rules are constraining because a person might be prevented from using a style that is more effective in that situation. For example, a supervisor might notice that the employee seems overly nervous playing a formal Employee Evaluation Meeting Game. The supervisor might decide to break out of the formal appraisal mode just to put the candidate more at ease. In fact, it's generally wise to begin these kinds of meetings by playing the Casual Conversation Game, thereby allowing for more informal topics and style choices.

Imagine the difficulty Janice must have faced in her first performance appraisal meeting with staff members who are both close friends and employees! She ultimately solved this problem in a very effective way: She told her staff that when they come to her office, she's "Janice the Leader." The topics and styles discussed in her office are focused on work-related issues. But when Janice comes to their individual desks, she's "Janice the Friend." The rule is this: Work-related games are held in Janice's office, and personal games are held in casual conversations at work desks. She set the rules, and they are working!

# Simple Steps for Playing Critical Conversation Games

Leadership is earned and clarified during critical conversations. A critical conversation is any kind of high-stakes exchange that involves an important decision, the communication of pivotal information or a problem-solving session in the face of a difficult challenge. Leaders have them all the time. Some are planned and intentional, while others are spontaneous and emotional. Yet leaders must be ready for these conversations, since followers pay a lot of attention to them. I certainly paid a lot of attention to what my father said when he had those father-son "talks" with my brother!

Followers listen because critical conversations reveal the leader's values, vision for the organization and skills for bringing problems into focus. Critical conversations are viewed as tests that leaders must win, over and over again, in order to build support from followers. Leaders who are new—like Janice was, in her supervisory role—have no history of conducting critical conversations. As a result, no one knew what Janice stood for, what she deemed important or where she wanted to lead the unit. Critical conversations define these things for everyone.

I recall several conversations I observed between a CEO of a major financial services institution and her executive team.

I remember one occasion in which she berated a team member for taking a risk on a critical project because it didn't work. Then, just a week later, in front of the same group of people, she lauded another team member for taking a risk that worked. These were conflicting messages about the value of risk-taking in the organization. It may be more complicated than that, but the followers got the clear message that risking is risky!

If impulsiveness and inconsistency don't work in critical conversations, what does work? What works is adopting a simple, systematic, disciplined approach to communicating: following some simple steps, every time, that are strategic and consistent. Below are the four simple steps of effective talk card play; the critical conversations featured in this book will use these rules to reveal how to take on the critical conversation challenges that define leadership.

## Step 1: Name the game

Name it; don't blow it off or run away from it. Some games are easy to name, like the New Employee Interview Game. These games have established scripts and rules that everyone knows. You may have trouble winning these games, but you know how to label them.

Other games are more difficult to name because they sneak up on you. For example, let's say you're playing the **Monday Morning Staff Meeting Game**. You are going through the agenda, catching up on projects—just like always. Then, one manager says, "We just can't seem to catch up on these projects. I'm not sure we're going in the right direction here. Maybe we should take a step back and assess."

At this point, that manager is clearly trying to initiate a new game—let's call it the **Vision Game.** As a leader, you should immediately see this comment as an attempt to play a new game. This new game is a test of your leadership. In fact, the other managers will probably look at you, the leader, to see your reaction to this comment. Your first reaction should be to name the game. To accurately name it, I would follow up with a simple question like, "What do you mean?" The manager's response will allow you to make some quick assessments:

- **What are the manager's goals?** If the manager's comment was made using a fairly friendly, low-power style, and the relationship of the manager to the leader is cooperative, then the manager's intention can be viewed as a genuine attempt to have a vision-based conversation.

- **Which cards is the manager playing—and which cards is the manager asking you to play?** If the manager's follow-up comment indicates that his or her goal is really cooperative, then the manager is continuing to play the Manager Card and is not challenging the Leader Card. If the comment was made as a challenge to your authority, then the manager is trying to switch cards and become the leader. When this person continues to play the Manager Card, he or she is asking you to continue to play the Leader Card.

- **What is the audience thinking?** Do others in the meeting want to switch from the Monday Morning Staff Meeting Game to the Vision Game? Is the timing right for that kind of discussion? If it's not appropriate at that point, then deflecting the manager's bid to change the game is best. If it is appropriate, then changing the game might be useful.

Failure to recognize a switch in the game can result in a major communication failure. If you shut down the manager and don't allow any follow-up elaborations on the comment, then you might miss out on an important opportunity to change the game and challenge the group with the Vision Game. If you play the Vision Game, and the others are willing to do that, it solidifies your role as leader. You passed an important test. You embraced the change and had a really effective conversation about vision that could benefit the organization.

Communication often fails because people mislabel the games they are playing. One person thinks it's one game, and the other thinks it's totally something else. A common example of this dilemma is the **Business Negotiation Game**. Because business deals often span continents, it's very common for cultures to clash during negotiations. Much has been written about U.S. business professionals trying to negotiate with Chinese or Japanese business associates. Before they developed some savvy in the international Business Negotiation Game, American business people would fly to Japan and begin meeting with Japanese executives looking to close a deal. Most Americans in business are accustomed to completing deals within two weeks or less, with intense negotiations over complex details.

Yet the Japanese, being people who are very focused on process, are more flexible with deadlines and prefer to get to know their partners thoroughly before making any business deals. In contrast, U.S. business people are typically more focused on outcome and immediate results. The fallout of these cultural differences is that in initial meetings, the Americans probably perceived that the Japanese were playing the Business Negotiation Game while the Japanese perceived that they were playing the Get Acquainted Game.

Consequently, while the Americans pushed for greater detail and immediate results, the Japanese wanted to focus only on the big picture, with a closing handshake instead of a contract.

In Card Talk terms, the Americans played their professional cards very differently in the Business Negotiation Game than the Japanese did in their reciprocal Get Acquainted Game. At the beginning, they didn't understand each other's cultural orientations and were not able to play the same kind of talk game to a successful conclusion.

## Step 2: Have simple goals

Don't try to do too much. Most games have simple goals and a clear understanding of what it takes to win. Approach critical conversations with this same "card game" mentality. For example, the goal of the Monday Morning Staff Meeting Game is simply to catch up on projects and schedules. Winning that game is accomplished when everyone feels fully informed for the week ahead. Everyone wants to leave the meeting winning that game.

It's useful to tell people what the goals are so they know what to expect. Research tells us that clear, simple goals that everyone understands are most likely to result in a win. Confusing people, shifting games or having ambiguous goals saps motivation. Clarity and simplicity engages people.

But what about the Vision Game? Let's say the manager wants to play that game, maybe in the middle of the Monday Morning Staff Meeting Game. The manager makes the comment, you ask for clarification, and it's clear the manager wants to switch the game and talk about vision—for the good of the group. Unfortunately, playing that game in the middle of the Monday Morning Staff Meeting Game will risk having everyone leave without being fully caught up—a game loss for everyone!

It's best to acknowledge that playing the Vision Game is a good idea. Yet timing is everything. See if the manager is willing to talk about that more complicated subject after everyone has caught up on the routine weekly planning. In other words, play one game at a time. Keep it simple. Finish one game successfully before starting another. Games have different rules, so when people start mixing games, it's difficult to win any of them. The Vision Game probably has more complicated rules and is certainly more difficult to win than is the Monday Morning Staff Meeting Game. Let's get the win with the first game and then move on to the second game. That's playing the Leader Card effectively—keeping people on track by letting everyone win the game they came to play. Then, if time allows, switch to a different game.

Of course, it's OK to take a brief break in the Monday Morning Staff Meeting Game and play some personal cards, to shift focus and increase engagement in the meeting. This might involve a story about a weekend activity or something fun. A few minutes playing the Friend Card and sharing a fun story with the group can break up the intensity and let people relax.

This shift is more of an engagement strategy, though, and not an abandonment of the original game. Moving to the Vision Game would involve a total switch to a more serious game, and therefore a moving away from the original purpose of the Monday Morning Staff Meeting Game.

## Step 3: Select the right cards

This last example illustrates a key principle in Card Talk: Talk games can only be won if everyone holds the cards that are capable of winning the game. What cards do you need in order to win the Monday Morning Staff Meeting Game? From your professional deck, you certainly need the Leader Card. The Leader Card keeps everyone on track, provides useful information and creates the structure needed to get the job done.

Sometimes, as in the last example, it's best to give people a break and get them engaged in something less serious. Initiating this can require playing the Friend Card, to talk about personal stories. It might also involve the Comedian Card, if a funny story is appropriate. The winning hand generally mixes cards from both personal and professional decks.

You explored your personal and professional decks in Chapter 1. Are you comfortable playing personal and professional cards in the same hand in a given game?

The point is, pick some cards from each pile every time. Leaders are expected to be personally engaged with followers. This means that people want leaders to be humans, not machines. Showing your personal cards in most games shows that you trust the people with whom you're communicating. It shows that you also want them to play a reciprocal personal card—for example, the Friend Card—and share personal information with you.

I have been known to play the Sports Fan Card at some meetings, to get people talking about an important game or one of their kid's sports stories. It gives people a break for a couple of minutes when needed.

A student recently shared a story with me about his commanding officer. This student is in the National Guard. His commanding officer had expressed to him, on several occasions, that he would like the soldiers in

*Play with no more than three cards in your hand at once.*

his command to speak up during meetings and briefings, to give their opinions about various things. Typically the officer comes into the meeting room, plays the Commanding Officer Card, and begins telling the troops about some issue. At the end, he says, "Any questions?"

Of course, there are never any questions because the reciprocal card to the Commanding Officer Card is the Soldier Card. The expectation is that the Soldier Card is all about listening and not about talking. If the commanding officer wants comments, the student told me that he would need to play another card to break out of that typical pattern.

Two additional points about card selection:

1. **Play with no more than three cards in your hand at once.** Again, keep it simple. When games have clear goals, people know what it takes to win. Your card choices should be similarly clear. Most games require only two or three cards to be successful. In the Monday Morning Staff Meeting Game, the Leader Card and perhaps the Sports Fan Card, or Friend Card, is all that's needed to win the game.

2. **Topics and styles should be clear and consistent.**
   Playing a card sets the expectation that you will or can
   talk about specific topics relevant to that card. The Leader
   Card in a specific area establishes the expectation that you
   will be an expert in that area and able to comment on
   a wide range of issues. Style choice should be consistent
   with the goals of the card. Generally, high friendliness, low
   formality and low power are most effective in winning
   friends.

## Step 4: Play to win

Don't give up too quickly! Many people will begin a talk
game and then just give up before anything meaningful can be
accomplished. This tendency is particularly true in critical conversations that some people like to avoid. A colleague of mine
is a supervisor. His job requires having performance appraisal
meetings with his direct reports. He hates doing them, so he
basically makes them about five minutes long. He only plays his
personal cards at these meetings so nothing related to the business gets done. That's not helping anyone.

How can you avoid this kind of self-defeating Card Talk play?
Plan your card play. Be clear about your business purpose. What
would you like to accomplish? What's the structure or the process needed for the critical conversation? What should you focus
on first, second, third? What cards would be useful to play?
Having answers to these questions will help you avoid giving up
too soon, or just avoiding the critical conversation altogether.

How can you assess the extent to which you have the communication style or approach necessary to hang in there and
play to win? Here are 10 items that determine the extent to
which you are focused on building a respectful working relationship with others while digging deeply into the subject matter of
the critical conversation.

## Communication Style Inventory

1 = Strongly Disagree, 2 = Disagree, 3 = No Opinion,
4 = Agree, 5 = Strongly Agree

| Communication Style Questions | Score |
|---|---|
| 1. I try to act in a friendly manner when facing a difficult conversation. | |
| 2. When in a difficult conversation I try to repeat back key points the other person says. | |
| 3. I seldom interrupt the other person during a difficult conversation. | |
| 4. I am extremely attentive to the other person's ideas. | |
| 5. I am an open communicator when communicating during difficult conversations. | |
| 6. I make sure to be well prepared on the issues before I discuss them. | |
| 7. In most difficult situations I explore the full range of issues. | |
| 8. I usually give many good reasons why the other person should accept my ideas. | |
| 9. I try not to rush to a conclusion before the issues have been explored. | |
| 10. I make a conscious effort to understand the other party's most important problems and issues. | |

The first five items of this survey focus on building relationships by being friendly, attentive and open as a communicator. If you scored above 15 in these five questions, you actively seek to build a stronger relationship out of the conversation. The second five items address your ability to understand the issues in the context of the other's most important problems. If your score is above 15 on these items, you can explore the full range of issues, develop them and creatively ensure they solve both parties' main concerns.

If your score is above 35 on this inventory, you are able to bring value to your card play. You have an engaging yet substantive approach to communicating. That's called "value-building," which is the goal of any communication encounter. Value is defined as solution over cost. If the solution selected to solve the problem goes beyond expectations in relation to price, then the solution has high value. In communication, it means that you are focused on building a successful relationship while also digging into the problem people are trying to solve.

Finally, let's talk about **listening**. As you can see from the first five items in this inventory, building a relationship with someone involves listening, or being attentive to the other's thoughts and showing that you understand what has been communicated. Listening takes place in three steps:

1. **Pay attention.** Develop eye contact and focus on what is being communicated. Avoid distractions and show that you care about what is being said. Others pick up very quickly on whether or not you care to understand.

2. **Acknowledge.** Vocally acknowledge that you understand. Pick out important words from the comments and repeat them back to the person. Again, show you really care about understanding.

3. **Follow up.** Don't change the subject. Ask a question or make a follow-up comment about what the person is talking about. Show respect for the subject matter.

Taking these steps satisfies each person's need for inclusion, control and affection, as indicated in Chapter 1. It shows respect, willingness to understand and engagement. Effective card play begins with listening. Rule No. 1 is all about understanding what's going on, and that can only be accomplished through effective listening.

Next, we turn to what's involved in creating the Leader Card.

# The Leader Card

Society pays a great deal of attention to leadership, and for good reason. Citizens look to their civic leaders to address their security and prosperity needs; employees look to their bosses for focus and direction in building a productive organization. In the previous three chapters, there have been several references to the Leader Card, so let's explore it in detail. We'll need it to understand how to play critical conversation games.

## What's Leadership?

Most people can point to a favorite leader—someone who really inspires them. For me that person was Mahatma Gandhi, who led the Indian people to independence from British rule. Gandhi paid attention to the substantive political issues of the day, which allowed him to craft very timely and effective political strategies to win Indian freedom. On the other hand, he was inspirational to the Indian people by casting off the bonds of colonial rule and refusing to submit to the British system that had become standard practice. He exhibited the rare combination of smarts, courage and sensitivity. He listened well and acted very decisively.

Perhaps the most useful definition of leadership comes from two authors who have explored it in a number of contexts—James Kouzes and Barry Posner, in their 2006 book, "*The Leadership Challenge*." They define leadership as "the art of mobilizing others to want to struggle for shared aspirations."

*Society pays a great deal of attention to leadership, and for good reason.*

The above definition recognizes that leadership is earned. It evolves out of the struggle for shared aspirations. When you bring something special to the table that others recognize as an advantage in the struggle, you earn both their respect and their commitment to follow and support. Leaders engage by listening, asking questions and providing information. When you are viewed as effective in helping win the struggle, your leadership is earned.

What expectations do followers have of leaders, so that leaders may sustain their position? Kouzes and Posner identify five:

1. **Challenge the process.** Many times, the endless stream of processes and procedures that people face in organizations can bog down real progress. Multiple systems that have outlived their original purpose may be cumbersome at best, or self-destructive at worst. Leaders need to constantly examine the systems and processes that impact productivity and performance and challenge those that are not working. Cutting through this red tape is difficult because most people like to do business the same way, year after year. When evidence surfaces that a system is not working, leaders are expected to do something about it.

2. **Inspire a shared vision.** Creating a clear vision should involve key stakeholders in the organization. This involvement sends the message that everyone owns the vision. The most important feature of the vision is that it provides a clear sense of direction for the organization. It provides clarity in a chaotic world. People know where they're going and why. That is very empowering to everyone.

3. **Enable others to act.** Leaders must be good at identifying talent, or what people excel at doing. Then they need to supply the resources that enable these individuals to do their jobs well. Leaders should certainly not get in the way, but should determine what will work to make the job and the environment most empowering for each individual. The implication is that the leaders know that everyone is different. What works for enabling one person may not work for another person. Understanding individual needs and working with them to create a more productive working environment is key!

4. **Model the way.** Followers expect that leaders will live by the same standards that the leaders have established for the organization. Kouzes and Posner recommend that leaders express their core values, which then become the standards that everyone should adopt in order to move the organization forward. This expression helps leaders find their voice and establish their credibility with everyone in the organization.

5. **Encourage the heart.** Finally, there is an emotional side to leadership. Leaders are responsible for helping everyone become emotionally attached to the vision of the organization, and ultimately to their specific jobs, in the course of achieving that vision. People are most productive when their heart is in their work. When people feel needed and that their work is significant, they are typically "all in." Also, when people perceive that the leader is really an approachable, personable individual

who can have normal, engaging conversations, they can relate better to the leader. Followers are most likely to open up to leaders they can get along with, as people.

Understand that leaders are always being judged by followers on these traits. The flip side is that leaders who rise up in the organization embrace this challenge and look for opportunities to assert or demonstrate their leadership. Why? Because they want to make a difference. They see what needs to be done. They accept the responsibility of helping others struggle for their shared aspiration of a well-run and effective organization that is moving in the right direction.

## Leader Card Inventory Survey

Now it's time to focus on *your* Leader Card. Think of a situation in which you served in a leadership role: work, sports, school, etc. Score yourself on the extent to which you demonstrated these behaviors in that role. Circle the number that best represents how often you performed these behaviors using this scale:

1 = Never      2 = Seldom      3 = Sometimes      4 = Often

## Challenging the Process

| | |
|---|---|
| 1.  Question assumptions underlying how the group worked | 1 2 3 4 |
| 2.  Offer solutions to problems the group faced | 1 2 3 4 |
| 3.  Share information across different groups in the organization | 1 2 3 4 |
| 4.  Have in-depth knowledge of how to accomplish the task | 1 2 3 4 |
| **Total Score** | |

## Inspiring a Shared Vision

| | |
|---|---|
| 5. Incorporate diverse ideas into the decision-making | 1 2 3 4 |
| 6. Seek the commitment of others to common goals | 1 2 3 4 |
| 7. Run meetings and make presentations effectively | 1 2 3 4 |
| 8. Communicate with outsiders to learn what they think | 1 2 3 4 |
| **Total Score** | |

## Enabling Others to Act

| | |
|---|---|
| 9. Articulate a clear vision of the road ahead | 1 2 3 4 |
| 10. Generate creative solutions to complex problems | 1 2 3 4 |
| 11. Show honesty and forthrightness in dealings with others | 1 2 3 4 |
| 12. Demonstrate a caring attitude toward others | 1 2 3 4 |
| **Total Score** | |

## Modeling the Way

| | |
|---|---|
| 13. Work to include all cultural and ethnic groups in the task | 1 2 3 4 |
| 14. Generate new resources to serve organizational goals | 1 2 3 4 |
| 15. Seek input from experts when necessary | 1 2 3 4 |
| 16. Exhibit a sense of humor | 1 2 3 4 |
| **Total Score** | |

## Encouraging the Heart

| | |
|---|---|
| 17. Demonstrate flexibility in responding to tough issues | 1 2 3 4 |
| 18. Consistently build on others' ideas in problem-solving discussions | 1 2 3 4 |
| 19. Step in and redirect destructive conflict | 1 2 3 4 |
| 20. Promote recognition of others' contributions | 1 2 3 4 |
| **Total Score** | |

## Add your scores using the following table:

| |
|---|
| Total for items 1-4, Challenging the Process: |
| Total for items 5-8, Inspiring a Shared Vision: |
| Total for items 9-12, Enabling Others to Act: |
| Total for items 13-16, Modeling the Way: |
| **Grand Total** |

Add your scores for each of the five "expectation" dimensions, and add your total score, as well. If you scored between 60 and 80 points, you have a great deal of confidence in your leadership skills; between 41 and 59, you are relatively unsure about your skills. If you scored between 20 and 40, you probably lack confidence.

Now look at your scores in each dimension. What was your highest score? Lowest? What do these differences mean? For example, if you had low scores on Challenging the Process and high scores on Encouraging the Heart, you may think of yourself as more of a social leader than a task facilitator.

# Leadership and Communication Style

Do you remember Chad from Chapter 1? He was the son of the boss and had a hard time taking over the business from his dad because he had trouble playing the Boss Card, or Leader Card. He was happy playing the Friend Card around employees, but did not have the voice of a leader.

One of Chad's issues was that his communication style impacted his ability to demonstrate these five leadership expectations, or traits. After completing a communication style inventory, it was clear that he wanted to pay more attention to relationship concerns with employees and less attention to developing the substantive issues of the business. As a result, he was less interested in challenging processes or inspiring a shared vision. He left those tasks to his dad.

Chad's comfort zone was focused on encouraging the hearts of employees and modeling the way. He had strong personal relationships with employees, and they all liked him on a personal level. Chad's focus was on making sure that people were happy and engaged, while also striving to be a role model for them.

On the other hand, Chad's dad was more issue-focused. His scores were several points higher in the "issue" area than in the "relationship" area. Chad's dad was more focused on challenging processes and crafting a future vision for the company because he was paying more attention to these leadership duties. He kept track of industry trends and was always looking for future business opportunities. Chad was more the insider/people guy.

Look at your scores. If they are relatively high in areas concerning both issues and relationships, then you stand the best chance of monitoring and acting upon all five leadership dimensions. In other words, if your Communication Style Inventory scores from Chapter 3 were relatively high in both areas, then your Leader Card Inventory Survey scores would probably also be high. You are likely to be encouraging and inspirational on the one hand and focused on challenging the process and crafting a new vision on the other hand.

# What Questions Do Leaders Ask?

What Chad will come to learn is that leadership is earned; it is not given. Even if someone is the designated boss, that person does not become a leader until followers agree to play the Follower Card. The moment followers anoint someone to help them struggle for shared aspirations is the point at which leadership, at least for that moment, is earned. As more people join this parade, the leadership becomes stronger.

Building the Leader Card begins by asking three critical questions:

1. **What needs to be done to make this place better?** The first question is the most important: What needs to be done? The company needs to grow, the team is here to win, and the nation must be free! How can these goals be achieved? The first job of a leader is to listen to others. What are the aspirations of the people? Gandhi, who led the Indian people out of British colonial rule, could not have led a march for freedom if people were not ready to fight for freedom. Gandhi listened intensely to the stories of oppression and heard yearnings for a better life and a future that breathed justice. He knew the people were ready and the time was right after many sessions spent listening to these stories.

2. **What can and should I do to make a difference?** After listening to and connecting with others, Gandhi decided that the first task in this struggle was to stop giving the British permission to oppress and to demand change. He decided that they could make a difference through nonviolent protests, boycotts and marches. Gandhi looked at his own skills and resources and decided that he had the ability, the courage and the motivation to do them. He never would have been successful if he had not first asked himself what he could do to make a difference.

3. **What should I say to keep the struggle visible and the path to success clear?** Leaders are communicators. They must continuously listen to others and talk to others. They must remain constantly visible to their followers in order to keep the vision real, maintain enthusiasm for the cause, and most importantly, to inspire. This is the key challenge in playing leadership games in organizations. Leaders have been granted the privilege of leading, and as a result, they must constantly be out front and in plain view of followers, encouraging them to move forward with the vision.

# Communication Strategies of Effective Leaders

Besides asking these questions, what else should be on the Leader Card? Followers expect leaders to use a variety of communication behaviors to motivate individuals. Here is a list of behaviors that research tells us are common on the Leader Card. Let's review the list and explore how specific behaviors promote leadership.

- **Identify problems.** Leaders examine the nature of the problem that needs to be solved and keep people on task while exploring it from many different perspectives.

- **Propose solutions.** Leaders have good suggestions for how to solve problems, and these suggestions should be creative and effective.

- **Seek information.** Remember that leaders are good at listening. They ask questions and listen to the answers. They don't change the topic to something they want to talk about; they let followers teach them how to lead. Shared aspirations drive leadership behaviors, so learning the followers' aspirations from every angle is key.

- **Give information.** People want leaders to be smart, and that usually means that leaders provide unique information about the challenges the group faces. Their unique perspectives are valued.

- **Structure the process of decision-making.** Leaders should challenge the process, but more importantly, they must build a new and better process for moving forward. If followers want new leadership, it's generally because the old leaders were stuck in a dysfunctional process of some kind.

- **Be active, but not pushy.** Leaders communicate and facilitate. They don't force people into compliance. Leaders who push are generally not effective. Leaders who listen and then act are much more effective. Remember, it's all about achieving a *shared* vision, not *your* vision.

# The Leadership Challenge

You can see what a challenge Chad had in developing the Leader Card. He had to essentially take over his dad's Leader Card while building on his own strength of playing the Friend Card with followers. Chad had a great deal of goodwill with employees, which is very important. Certainly, creating and sustaining the Leader Card is a tall order for anyone.

But, that's what this book is about. Effective leaders, like Gandhi, build their leadership one critical conversation at a time. It's not done in some grandiose manner in which someone is suddenly appointed to a leadership role and people automatically get in line behind that person. Leadership takes a long time to be earned. It is the accumulation of trust and confidence that emerges from effective critical conversations over months and even years.

Given the importance of executing critical conversations effectively, where can you start? It's best to start by understanding the Casual Conversation Game. The following chapter will provide the basics for you to begin earning the Leader Card.

# Part 2:
# Critical Conversation
# Games

# The Casual Conversation Game

I was talking to a group of supply chain executives in a workshop one day, and I asked this important question: "How many of you are afraid of having critical conversations with employees—or even with family members?" Out of the group of 40, about half raised their hands.

I was not surprised to see so many hands go up. Studies show that most people are afraid of critical conversations—those that take place during performance appraisals, while running a meeting or giving a presentation. Most people are fine with casual conversations, but when the topic gets serious, they clam up or just try to get through the matter as quickly as possible.

I then asked the executives why they were fearful. The consensus was that critical conversations are tense because they can occasionally result in conflict. Some of these conversations are about employee performance, which can put an employee on the defensive; others are about resources and how best to do a job. The basic fear is that serious conversations can sometimes turn negative, with people getting defensive.

# The Role of Identity in Critical Conversations

I told the group of executives that we need to first understand what, specifically, drives the threatening nature of critical conversations. Once we understand the triggers, we can play the right cards with the best topics and styles that will prevent us from pulling these triggers.

Perhaps the biggest trigger in critical conversations is individual identity. As we know from the first chapter, every critical conversation interaction puts two important elements in play. First, we have a job to do: We have a topic to discuss and a problem to solve. We exchange messages for that purpose, whatever it is. Second, our identity is in play. All of us want to play the cards that are most able to make both parties look good, so we can be respected.

In casual conversation, our identity is also in play, but it is generally not threatened by the topics, which are low-risk. We are not being formally evaluated or pushed around in any sense. It's easy interaction.

This is not the case in critical conversations. These conversations have a goal, and identity is particularly important in this goal, as both people want to solve a problem and win. They're serious. The cards people show, the topics they present and the style choices they make matter. Because identities are front-and-center, people pay extra attention to styles. Is the level of friendliness, formality and power appropriate? Is the other person respecting me for who I am?

If any person perceives that the cards, topics or styles are inappropriate, for whatever reason, then that person's identity is threatened. He or she feels disrespected (positive face violations), not listened to, not included or pushed into doing things they object to doing (negative face violations). That's when the focus of the conversation turns from problem-solving to conflict. Let me illustrate this with what I call the **Communication Games Triangle.**

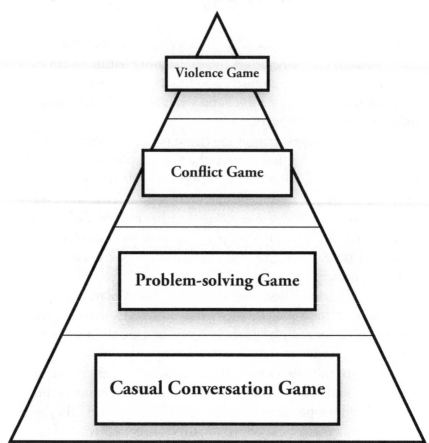

At the lowest level of the Communication Games Triangle is the Casual Conversation Game. This is where we spend most of our time, as communicators. It's aimed largely at building relationships, while sharing values and insights about issues. At this level, I like to tell stories about my daily experiences and my family. As we will see later, our ability to effectively interact with people on a professional level relies heavily on the quality of this (seemingly ordinary) casual conversation.

At some point, perhaps in a meeting or in the course of sharing information, people might redefine the Casual Conversation

Game as a problem-solving activity. Problem-solving involves taking on a specific task or problem and working toward completing it.

Critical conversations often begin as a casual conversation that unexpectedly becomes the Problem-solving Game. Have you ever talked with the boss at a social gathering, in a casual interaction—like the Sports Talk Game—that evolved into the Business Discussion Game? When the more serious, Problem-solving Game emerges, people want to sound engaged and insightful—and to project a strong identity.

The key point is that during the Problem-solving Game, the task and identity elements are about equally important. Communicators are playing cards to provide competent input, which keeps their identities at the forefront of the interaction. They are also working to solve the problem, which keeps the task element in play.

As a result, the defining characteristic of problem-solving is that identity and task are prominently in play but relatively balanced. One does not typically dominate the other, which allows everyone to focus on the job at hand. In fact, the Problem-solving Game involves disagreement, but in a way that is not identity-threatening for the communicators.

During critical conversations, on the other hand, people raise topics or use styles that can threaten identities. Often, this happens unintentionally: Perhaps a nonverbal gesture was a little too intense; perhaps the topic was too personal; maybe someone was interrupted while making a key point, which was viewed as offensive. Whatever the source, once a person's positive or negative face has been threatened, he or she feels the need to select topics and styles aimed at restoring face. When communication is focused on restoring positive or negative face, people cross the line from playing the Problem-solving Game to playing the Conflict Game.

Conflict is focused exclusively on identity or face restoration. The problem-solving focus starts to melt away. Individuals devote their energy to repairing or supporting their face needs, so that they can once again look competent and make it clear that they can't be pushed around.

This jump to conflict and face restoration often happens very quickly. People find themselves in conflict and they are not sure why. "Was it something I said?" is what we often hear. Remember our poor friend Philip, who played the Salesperson Card with his daughter? She started the conversation with her dad about a problem she was having at school. Rather than listening to the problem and staying in the problem-solving mode, he interrupted her and told her how to solve her problem.

That lack of listening to her perspective of the situation—a high-power move by Philip—denied his daughter the freedom to communicate, and thus challenged her negative face needs. She got angry instantly. The conversation morphed immediately into the Conflict Game, and Philip did not understand why. Remember: He was hampered by his trained incapacity because he played that same card with everyone. But everyone is *not* a client—especially his daughter!

Finally, as people play more deeply into the Conflict Game, they can begin playing the Violence Game. More time spent playing the Conflict Game often results in additional frustration, because communicators are trying to restore their identity with words—and it's not working. People become frustrated and start to feel that the only way to control the other communicator is through mental, or even physical, violence.

Much research reveals that violence is caused by a lack of ability to restore identity with words. Violence prevention is all about reducing identity threats and finding ways that people can express their identities with words—without having to resort to violence. It's moving away from playing the Violence Game, back into the Conflict Game, and then ultimately into the Problem-solving Game.

# Bouncing in and out of Problem-solving and Conflict

What happens in most critical conversations is that people bounce back and forth between playing the Problem-solving Game and the Conflict Game. I was talking recently with Dustin, a graduate student in one of my courses. Dustin is a full-time employee of a large manufacturing firm, and he revealed during a group task that he did not care very much for his immediate supervisor. I asked what he didn't like about him. Dustin replied that during meetings (critical conversations), his boss would be fine, and then—all of a sudden—he would insult someone (positive face violation). Supporters of the person being attacked would then rally to defend the individual, which detoured the meeting.

In other words, Dustin did not like the Conflict Game. He felt that it was unproductive. For the most part, when people focus only on identity restoration, they can't focus on problem-solving. On the flip side, however, a little bit of conflict can sometimes be useful in problem-solving, as long as it's managed well.

I recall a conflict that originated in small-claims court that I had videotaped for research purposes. The conflict was mediated after two women, Beth and Ann, had agreed to allow a mediator to help them. They began accusing each other of wrongdoing, with each playing the Victim Card in the Conflict Game. Positive and negative face attacks were flying around, along with some yelling.

Finally, based on the way they were talking to each other, the mediator remarked that she believed Beth and Ann knew each other very well, on a personal level. The women agreed that they were once best friends, but that Beth had caught Ann sleeping with her boyfriend and had become angry. At that point, the two women started talking about old times and each began playing the Friend Card, once again. They went from playing the

Conflict Game to playing the Casual Conversation Game very quickly. Ann and Beth then started crying and saying that they missed each other, agreeing that the former boyfriend (of both women) was a jerk.

When the mediator asked about the small-claims problem, Beth, the accuser, agreed to drop it, but Ann volunteered to pay. The Problem-solving Game was brief and effective because the two had spent some time playing the Conflict Game, which had resulted in the restoration of their identities as friends, and not enemies. The point is that sometimes, playing the Conflict Game can energize a problem-solving activity by clearing the air. The mediator was effective in moving the women's argument in this direction.

Now we come back to our original purpose for introducing the Communication Games Triangle. Recall that many people are afraid of critical conversations because they can escalate into conflict. That's true, but if you can support the other party's face needs on a repeated basis throughout the conversation, then for the most part, people will play the Problem-solving Game. But you may still be afraid of the possibility of going into the conflict zone because you are an apprehensive communicator when it comes to critical conversations.

Complete items in the following survey to get a greater sense of how apprehensive you are about participating in critical conversations.

## Communication Apprehension Survey

Indicate the extent to which these items are true about you by choosing a number between 1 and 5.
1 = Strongly Disagree, 2 = Disagree, 3 = No Opinion, 4 = Agree, 5 = Strongly Agree

| Communication Apprehension Items | Score 1-5 |
|---|---|
| 1. When talking with a new friend, I feel nervous. | |
| 2. I don't like to speak up around my friends. | |
| 3. I am often tense and nervous in normal conversations. | |
| 4. I often go out of my way to avoid casual conversations. | |
| 5. My friends think I am quiet. | |
| 6. I dislike participating in critical conversations. | |
| 7. I don't like to speak up in a group discussion. | |
| 8. I am often tense and nervous when difficult topics are discussed. | |
| 9. I usually let others do the talking in critical conversations. | |
| 10. My friends say I tend to avoid critical conversations. | |
| **Total Communication Apprehension Survey Score** | |

Items 1-5 focus on your level of interest in engaging others in conversation. If you scored above 15 on these items, you are generally more interested in keeping to yourself. If you scored below 10 on these items, you like to engage people.

Items 6-10 focus on your interest in engaging in critical conversations in groups of three or more people. If you scored higher than 15 on these items, you are apprehensive about having critical conversations with others. A score below 10 means that you are willing to engage when needed, and you probably see the advantage of having these conversations.

# The Casual Conversation Game

## Step 1: Name the game

You can probably tell by now that the Casual Conversation Game plays an important role in effectively setting up a critical conversation. In other words, it's difficult to have a critical conversation without first having a casual conversation, or a history of casual conversations. Casual conversation creates the foundation upon which problem-solving and conflict evolves.

How do you know when you're having a casual conversation with someone? Can you name the game? The difficulty with casual conversation is that it can quickly move to some other game, like the Conflict Game. You're talking about something by just sharing opinions, with no particular goal in mind, and someone starts insulting (intentionally or unintentionally) someone else—and the Conflict Game breaks out.

The goal is to be mindful of the need for casual conversation that allows people to connect in a friendly and constructive way. Some people tell a story about something at work (Storytelling Game). Others chat about family events (Family Disclosure Game). These are valuable exchanges, and are really about building relationships with people.

## Step 2: Have simple goals

The key to winning the Casual Conversation Game lies in keeping it casual and fun, so both parties: a) build a relationship; b) establish their identities; and c) create communication rules for interacting. Let's look at each of these individually, and then how they work together.

**Building a relationship.** Did you ever notice that when strangers chat in an elevator, they almost always talk about the weather? That's because it's a safe topic that they can use to build a relationship. We want to gather some really important information quickly: How much do I like this person, and how much can I trust this person? When we graduate from "the weather" to some other, more personal topic, trust and affiliation start to grow.

Obviously, the more we interact, the more information we have about the relationship and what it means. If we stick with topics that are not very personal, we might define ourselves as "acquaintances." If the topics become more personal, we might say we're "friends." The Casual Conversation Game helps fill in the blanks about the kind and depth of relationships we share with others.

**Establishing identities.** While we're forming a relationship in casual conversation, we're also trying to project how we want others to see us. What cultural identity is important? What social or group identity do we want others to associate with us? What kind of unique personal qualities do we want others to understand?

Jodie, one of my workshop participants, recently expressed frustration about not breaking into the executive ranks of her company. I looked at how she was projecting herself, and it was not in a very professional manner. Her dress, hair and makeup suggested that she was playing the Provocative Female Card, and not the Colleague Card. After admitting this was the case, she thought about what a more professional appearance might look like.

Remember, it's probably during casual conversation—which is generally the first time you interact with someone—that a first impression is created. The point is to be deliberate in the kind of identity that you want to create, and then work to acquire and play the associated cards.

**Creating communication rules**. Think of rules as the habits people form when they talk. What topics and styles are people used to sharing? How much should each person talk? How long should each person talk? Can big words and long sentences be used, or just small words and short sentences? Is proper grammar needed? May this person curse? This is just a small sample of the kinds of rules that people create while playing the Casual Conversation Game.

Casual conversation rules are formed when people make topic or style choices while playing their cards and others simply accept those choices by reciprocating them. For example, when someone plays the Leader Card by talking about vision issues using very formal language, and listeners reciprocate by sharing their vision ideas with formal language, the listeners are agreeing to play the Follower Card in response to the Leader Card. This not only shows support for what the leader is doing, but creates informal rules about what topics and styles are appropriate.

If the leader also plays the Friend Card and tells a personal story with very friendly, informal and low-power styles, and others reciprocate with the Friend Card and similar styles, they are again showing support for the leader's choices and creating informal rules about topics and styles.

Generally, these rules carry over from casual conversation into problem-solving. Once we develop a relationship and establish an identity with someone, these rules start to stabilize. People rely on these rules to share information during subsequent encounters.

## Step 3: Select the right cards

Once the game has been defined and all players know that casual conversation is happening, they can begin to pick their talk cards. Certainly, most cards in casual conversations come from personal decks. If you took an in-depth inventory of your personal deck, what would you find?

The answer comes from the inventory exercise in Chapter 1. Are you comfortable playing the Friend Card or the Acquaintance Card? Playing these cards requires you to share personal topics that might be difficult for you to share. If you had a high score on the Communication Apprehension Survey at the beginning of this chapter, then you're probably challenged to pull out the Friend Card in a casual conversation.

If you find playing the Friend Card or Acquaintance Card challenging, then you might want to think about topics you are willing to share with people you trust. Everyone has an interesting personal story to share. Perhaps the Sports Fan Card would get you started. What are some of the personal cards you identified in Chapter 1 that you might like to play in telling a personal story? Learn the benefits of playing the Casual Conversation Game!

## Step 4: Play to win

Winning the Casual Conversation Game involves the building of interpersonal relationships that allows parties to better understand one another in terms of preferences, values, beliefs and attitudes. This information becomes invaluable when the stakes get higher in critical conversation.

Sara came in to see Jennifer, her team leader, for her annual performance evaluation. Jennifer looked at Sara and said, "Oh, you're the one with long hair." Clearly, Jennifer did not know Sara as an individual, unique from any other person on the team. They did not have a relationship; Jennifer had no idea what kind of identity needs Sara had, and the pair had not established useful communication rules for guiding their interaction. The evaluation went as expected. Jennifer looked down at her form, said a few things, and then dismissed Sara. It took about five minutes—not very meaningful. Sara probably left feeling worse about herself and the company.

This was an opportunity for Sara's boss to have a critical conversation. As a result, neither person won this game, because neither benefitted. They lost because they did not know each other interpersonally. Jennifer could have at least used the time to get to know Sara better.

The point is that critical conversations are built on a foundation that is created by many plays of the Casual Conversation Game. Taking the time to have these social interactions is important in order for the team to function productively. Leaders must encourage these conversations and have them regularly. If leaders model the way in this area, the whole organization will benefit.

# The Decision-making Game

How many times have you sat in a meeting, wondering where the meeting was going? Try to put yourself in Kayla's shoes, as she attended a department retreat to focus on strategic planning. As the group went round and round on some trivial point, she looked down at the table and thought, "Are we going to get anything done?" She was frustrated!

Kayla blamed the leader, and rightfully so. Her boss failed to play the Leader Card by not challenging the process and moving things forward in a timely fashion. That started a chain reaction that caused the group members to check out. We know from the last chapter that we expect leaders to take charge in meetings, but sometimes they don't.

## Step 1: Name the game

In Chapter 5, we talked about the Casual Conversation Game, and we contrasted it with the Problem-Solving Game. Interaction escalates to the problem-solving level when the need arises to move forward on a specific issue. The goal in problem-solving is to keep focused on the substantive concerns facing the group, while avoiding the Conflict Game. To achieve this goal, let's begin by talking about what an effective Decision-making Game looks like. Here are the five features of effective decision-making:

1. **The leader insists on understanding all important aspects of the problem.** When exploring any major decisions, it is vitally important to break down all relevant aspects of the problem and get really good information about all of these elements, so their impact on the decision can be assessed.

2. **The team develops criteria for making an acceptable choice to solve the problem.** What makes one choice better or worse than another? For example, what might companies look for when deciding which supplier to select for a specific project? Relevant criteria might include quality of work, price, delivery timeframe and service reputation. Failure to develop criteria often results in an impulsive choice that works out poorly in the long run.

3. **The team finds a range of good choices that meet these criteria.** Once the criteria are set it's best to find several choices that fit. Companies are wise to find several suppliers that are qualified to do work for the company. Getting a bid from just one supplier limits the company's ability to apply the criteria and decreases the chances of finding a good fit.

4. **The team explores the pluses and minuses of the alternatives.** After lining up the options, which ones look best? The optimal strategy is to rigorously apply the criteria and then rank-order the options. We know from research that people are more determined to avoid an option with just one negative consequence even if the other options have only weak positive consequences. This bias is not realistic, though; the careful weighing of factors almost always produces a better choice.

5. **The team selects the best alternative and sticks with it.** Finally, after weighing all the alternatives, the team picks

an option (probably the one with the fewest negative consequences) and commits to it by agreeing to follow through. Think of the last time you made a big decision. How would you grade your decision-making process? Did you walk through each of the first four steps before making your choice?

Walking through these five steps is the best way to play the group-wide **Decision-making Game**. But are groups always best for making decisions?

Gary is a manager working in an automotive logistics firm. He expressed his frustrations to me about working with groups to make decisions. In one recent training session, he remarked, "Groups take too much time. I can make a better decision myself in less time. Why mess with a group?"

There are probably a couple of factors in play with this kind of reaction. First, some people are uncomfortable playing the Leader Card. Gary falls into that group. He was promoted from the ranks to his manager position, and he prefers just getting the job done by himself, like he did when he was not a manager.

Second, Gary doesn't like meetings, and neither do his direct reports. Since he doesn't like meetings, he doesn't want to think about how to make them more productive. After giving Gary some tips on how to better run a meeting, Gary felt more open to meeting with his team on important issues.

I also pointed out to Gary that research makes it clear: *Groups typically make better decisions than individuals working alone.* Real-world groups performing work-related tasks almost always perform better than the best-performing individual in the group. Certainly, Gary should not meet on every issue. When important decisions must be made, he should put his fears and frustrations aside. Playing the group-wide Decision-Making Game well often produces a better outcome.

## Step 2: Have simple goals

What tips did Gary receive that gave him a checklist of how to make meetings more productive? Here are five factors that boost group performance:

1. **Clear group goals.** People should meet to accomplish specific, clear goals. At least some of these goals should be focused on making a decision of some kind. Meeting to just share information is often frustrating because information can be shared more efficiently through document-sharing or email. Clear goals provide focus, are efficient and are very motivating. When Gary was asked about his biggest obstacle in having productive meetings, it came down to not having clear goals. People met to share information and it got boring quickly.

2. **An effective size and sufficient time.** When groups become too large for the task they have to perform, they become ineffective. Group sizes ranging from three to eight allow for more open communication and a freer flow of information. Plus, it's just easier to schedule a smaller number of people to get together and discuss the problem. The key is to give the group sufficient time to make decisions using the outline above. Rushing can cut off productive communication.

3. **Engaging discussion.** Since Gary thought meetings were inherently boring, so did everyone else. What can be done to make meetings more interesting? A good place to start is to begin the meeting with something fun or interesting, to get the group talking openly. We're not talking about formal reports here, but throwing out a topic that the group would enjoy discussing for a couple of minutes.

4. **Open communication.** When people feel free to bounce ideas off one another in an open and accepting fashion, the final group product will improve. Disagreement is important as long as it's constructive and does not attack personal identities—that can thrust people into

the Conflict Game. The leader should make it clear that all ideas are welcome and valued. Interruptions should be banned. Listening to and then following up on the speaker's ideas should be actively enforced.

5. **A culture of trust and respect.** The culture of the group can have a dramatic impact on the willingness of members to participate. Establishing trust, or the perception that others are acting in one another's best interests, enables everyone to contribute freely and openly. A good indication that trust is low is the formation of cliques or coalitions. These small groups that gang up on others can quickly foster mistrust and disrespect.

## Evaluate Your Meetings

Now it's time to evaluate your team meetings. Select two meetings to evaluate—one that was successful and provided an enjoyed experience, and one that was unsuccessful and perhaps fell apart or had a bad outcome. Name the meetings below and check whether each meeting did or did not display the factors listed in the table.

Good meeting: _____

Bad meeting: _____

## Qualities of the Meetings

| Did this meeting ... | Good Meeting | Bad Meeting |
|---|---|---|
| 1. Explore all aspects of the problem? | | |
| 2. Develop criteria for selecting options? | | |
| 3. Create a range of options? | | |
| 4. Assess the positives and negatives of the options? | | |

| Did this meeting ... | Good Meeting | Bad Meeting |
|---|---|---|
| 5. Select the best alternative? | | |
| 6. Have the right number of members? | | |
| 7. Establish clear group goals? | | |
| 8. Have everyone engaged? | | |
| 9. Open communication? | | |
| 10. A willingness to disagree? | | |
| 11. Sufficient time to problem solve? | | |
| 12. A culture of trust and respect? | | |
| 13. Celebrate its success? | | |
| **Total Check Marks** | | |

Do you have more check marks for the successful meeting? In theory, the good meeting should have many more check marks. If the numbers are about the same for both meetings, then you might want to rethink the criteria you use to define success. For example, maybe you thought a meeting was successful if it seemed like fun or if you liked the outcome, looking back on it. Generally, groups that pay more attention to the process of group communication perform better.

## Step 3: Select the right cards

Certainly an effective Leader Card is needed to win the Decision-making Game. We have discussed the kinds of topics and styles a leader needs to run a good meeting. We'll continue to explore the Leader Card throughout this book.

What other cards should the leader display in moving along a meeting? One or two other professional and personal cards would be useful. For example, the Friend Card or the Acquaintance Card would be useful to play on occasion, to share personal information during casual conversation. These cards promote relationship-building, since others would be asked to reciprocate these cards and would also share personal information.

From the professional deck, the leader might show the Expert Card or the Colleague Card during the meeting. Leaders are expected to provide expert information from time to time, and to act as colleagues with others in the meeting. These cards promote a team atmosphere and allow individuals to freely exchange information.

## Step 4: Play to win

What prevents people from winning the Decision-making Game? So far, we've talked about what makes groups perform well. Mostly, these ideas focus on making sure meetings are both fun and structured. What are some of the more common problems that can throw off a meeting? What are some pitfalls that make the Decision-making Game fail? Consider these 10 potholes:

**Pothole 1: Unclear or controversial tasks.** Meetings are more difficult when they focus on controversial or emotional topics, like values, or when the need for a specific decision disappears. Only when the group's task is specific or factual, and everyone is clear on what is needed, does the group perform well. When only a few people know what's going on, the meeting collapses.

**Pothole 2: Low leadership participation.** If the leader does not participate in the interaction and lets the group do what it wants, the meeting usually falls apart. Leaders must have an agenda that outlines the decisions to be made as well as how they should be made. Leaders must promote open communication while staying actively engaged throughout the meeting.

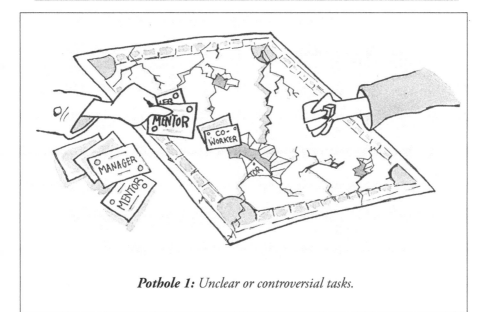

***Pothole 1:*** *Unclear or controversial tasks.*

**Pothole 3: Pushy leadership.** The opposite of passive leadership is pushy leadership. Pushy leaders try to make the group come to the decision the leader wants—which is not necessarily the best decision. When group members like, trust and respect each other, they are more likely to occasionally play the Friend Card. If the Friend Card is played at appropriate moments, when everyone wants to take a break and play a social game, then group sentiment grows and people feel better about being in the group. If the leader allows too much time for the Casual Conversation Game, though, the group has difficulty completing the task.

**Pothole 4: Leaders who lack compassion.** People expect leaders to play the Friend Card from time to time. The leader should be viewed as a normal person who has a personal life like everyone else. Leaders who are not available personally tend not to be trusted by followers. Letting some of the personal side show helps promote a trusting climate, and ultimately, group cohesiveness.

**Pothole 5: Group size.** Leaders should strive for the "Goldilocks" group size. Groups that are too large are difficult to manage—people tend to drift off and not participate. On the other hand, small groups might lack the insight needed to take on a significant challenge. The key is to find just the right size group for the task. One recommendation is to begin an important task with a small group that can work quickly and efficiently. Then their product can be taken to the larger group, for consideration. This two-stage process usually works well.

**Pothole 6: Cultural insensitivity.** Some ethnic cultures, as you may have experienced, don't like controversy or the sharing of different opinions. As a result, they are more likely to avoid the open discussion that is often needed for the group to sort out its differences and find a productive path. If the group is faced with a difficult challenge, people from some ethnic cultures may be unwilling to confront this challenge. The leader needs to figure out a way to engage these individuals so that their views can be heard.

**Pothole 7: Lack of fact checking.** When the information and opinions of group members are closely scrutinized—as opposed to building a reliance on only cursory examination—groups are likely to be much more effective. Not checking facts or allowing people to make grand leaps in logic without asking for documentation often results in poor decision-making, because the information has low quality.

**Pothole 8: Rushing to judgment.** Perhaps the biggest challenge for groups is rushing through the process. Groups get impatient and want to take shortcuts, and that generally means closing off discussion prematurely. If no one develops clear decision criteria and viable options that meet these criteria, then all the options look alike—there's no way to tell which one is better.

**Pothole 9: Choosing impulsively.** A consequence of rushing to judgment is being impulsive: making an emotional decision. Decisions should be made with facts and verified opinions. If the group lets members make assumptions on the basis of wild speculation, rumor or invalid inferences, then group decision-making suffers. Try to imagine how an objective third party might evaluate your decisions. Would this person agree that your decisions are based on high-quality facts and not speculation?

**Pothole 10: Allowing influential members to raise irrelevant topics.** The leader's job is to keep the team on task. Sometimes, influential members will challenge the leader by trying to take over the meeting through irrelevant topics, or by hurrying the group to a quick decision. Going against these influential members can be difficult. Effective task leaders ask questions, they know what important information to continuously bring back to the group, and they keep the group on task.

# Steering Around the Potholes

The best way to steer around these potholes is to follow the structure outlined above. It's called "staying in your lane." The leader's lane is guiding the process, summarizing along the way to ensure that everyone see the progress being made. It's pulling the group along a productive path regardless of the challenges: a pushy member, an emotional outburst calling for quick action, failure to gather and reliance on the evidence.

Gary had all of these challenges as a logistics manager. One of the members of his team, Eric, was a former military officer. Eric was constantly talking about how the military did it better. Gary said he talked with Eric privately about this behavior. Gary learned that Eric really wanted a leadership role of some kind on the team. Gary decided to give him a key responsibility and to bring his thinking to the team during meetings. That responsibility turned things around. Eric was able to influence the group in a specific capacity and was no longer disruptive in other matters. It was a win-win for everyone.

The point is that steering around potholes often requires some creativity. A leader learns how to gather information, thinks things through and takes the time to reflect and make a decision. As we know from the last chapter, leaders understand the needs of followers and will figure out a collective path forward. The Decision-making Game turns out to be a key marker of how others evaluate a leader's competence. Be disciplined, and do it well.

# The Driving-change Game

Do you remember Chad from Chapter 1? He took over the family business and wanted to make some changes. These changes were difficult because he had not yet won the right to play the Boss Card with employees: They still viewed him as the son of the boss, and not yet really in charge. The solution for Chad was to stop consistently playing the Friend Card and start playing the Boss Card—slowly at first, and then more frequently, as employees responded positively to it.

Playing the right card is only part of the story, though. The rest of the story is figuring out how to structure the change process and which cards to play in each individual critical conversation. The Driving-change Game is a version of the Problem-solving Game. The problem, as Chad described it, is building a culture of change that makes it easier for an organization to move forward and compete. Many companies struggle with this issue because they spend all their time working within their legacy systems, just to get work out the door. Nevertheless, innovating and moving forward is required now more than ever.

## Step 1: Name the game

To begin, what do we know about change?

For most people, change is very difficult. Why? Because it's easier to keep doing what we're used to doing. Changing a habit, or a way of doing something that seems to work, often doesn't make sense to people.

People are more likely to embrace change when they are convinced that the old ways don't work anymore. Consider Keith, a software executive who loved greasy food. After a mild heart attack, Keith finally realized that he had to lose weight and get healthy—or else. His doctors had previously told him that he had to stop eating greasy food and start exercising, but it took an emergency to get him to listen to this message and make a change.

Do you need an emergency, like losing a big client or seeing your revenues decline suddenly, in order to change? Or are you willing to shift gears on your own when faced with good reasons to change? Remember, leaders ask what needs to be done and what they can do to make things better. They don't wait for crises. They see crisis coming and take action or change direction to avoid disaster.

We know from research that it's a lot easier to get people to start doing something they've never done before than it is to stop them from doing something they are accustomed to doing. In fact, research tells us that it's three times easier for people to start doing something new than it is to stop doing an old habit. For Keith, it was much harder to stop eating greasy food—he switched to salads—than to start exercising. He was really fond of his old food habits, so changing those was difficult. It was easier to convince him to start walking a few days a week.

We also know that people differ regarding their openness to change. About half the population accepts change and falls into two categories—**innovators** and **early adopters**. Innovators embrace change. They are emotionally tied to trying new things and telling others about it. Just below them are early adopters. These people like change, but are more rational about it. They are more concerned with the practical value in the change, but are still open to it.

The remaining half of the population rejects change. The **late adopters** will only change when they have to, for some specific reason—perhaps they can't buy the old stuff anymore, because it isn't sold. They are forced to buy the new stuff. At the bottom of the change barrel are the **laggards**. They hate change and actively fight it. My mother would not give up her videocassette recorder (VCR), even after VCR tapes were no longer being sold.

Ask yourself: What is your approach to change? Answer the questions below, and determine how much you like change.

## Assessing Your Adopter Type

What kind of adopter are you? Answer these 10 questions to get a feel for the approach you like to use when confronting change. Score each item on a scale of 1 to 5.

1 = Strongly Disagree, 2 = Disagree, 3 = Unsure, 4 = Agree,
5 = Strongly Agree

| Adopter Type Opinions | Score |
|---|---|
| 1. I like to learn about the latest computer technologies. | |
| 2. If I could afford it, I would buy the latest and greatest cell phone. | |
| 3. I always keep an open mind about trying new things. | |
| 4. I like telling others about the new things I have purchased. | |
| 5. My friends are very technology-oriented. | |
| 6. When my friends have something new and different, I like to check it out. | |
| 7. I come from a family of innovators. | |
| 8. Change is easy for me. | |

| Adopter Type Opinions | Score |
|---|---|
| 9. I have little patience for people who don't like to try new ideas. | |
| 10. People often come to me for advice about new technologies. | |
| **Total Score:** | |

If your score is between 35 and 50, you are probably an **innovator.**

If your score is between 25 and 34, you are probably an **early adopter.**

If your score is between 20 and 24, you are probably a **late adopter.**

If your score is between 10 and 19, you are probably a **laggard.**

Are you surprised about your score? If you are under age 35, you are probably an early adopter or innovator. If you have an advanced college degree, you may also fall into one of these categories: The fact that you went to college likely means that you are able to take risks and are open to change. However, you may have a lower score and believe that change is about fashion and fads. Change should have a rationale to justify shifting course in some way.

We know from research that people need lots of information when change is coming. First, they need to be informed about the change, because it is going to cause anxiety. Lack of information about the change simply adds to that anxiety. The information must be clear, consistent and frequent. Not informing people will sabotage the change rather quickly.

Second, people like to participate in the process of making the change happen and making it successful. Not only do they want to be consulted about it, but they also want feel like a team taking on a new challenge.

Playing the Leader Card and driving change means understanding the most effective process for directing change, as well as deciding which cards to play to make that happen. Let's turn first to understanding the process of effective change.

## Step 2: Have simple goals

Think of it this way: Leading change is the process of guiding a series of steps that gradually move people in the desired direction. Implementing these steps can be frustrating because leaders generally want change faster than followers do. Here are four simple goals that are most productive when thinking about and driving change.

**Goal 1: Readiness.** How ready are people for change? What is their frame of mind, their level of interest, and their understanding of the technical issues related to the change? We have already covered the issue of what kinds of people are most interested in change: innovators and early adopters. They embrace the mindset that change is necessary and desirable, even if the old ways are working. "How can things be done better?" is a question they would ask.

Even if, as individuals, some people are ready for change, it doesn't mean that the whole group embraces it. I recall talking with Emily, a recent hire on a sales team. She had been trained by her previous employer on all of the new customer relations management (CRM) software by her previous employer and found it very useful in saving time, reducing mistakes and creating sales leads. Yet when she tried to introduce CRM to her fellow team members, they thought it was unnecessary and too complicated. What they had been doing for 20 years was working fine, they thought.

Emily ran into a brick wall because her team was not ready for change. She introduced a solution to a problem that the team didn't realize it had. Before even talking about CRM, Emily should have focused on the problems with the old sales system. She could have shown the team how the old system wastes time, is difficult to update and does not create sales leads.

After demonstrating these problems in a convincing manner, the group might have been more open to change.

The key point is that change advocates, like Emily, must first understand the attitudes and values of the people they are targeting for change. Are they ready, as individuals and as a team, for something different? Do they see the need for change? If not, how can the change leader get them ready?

**Goal 2: Engagement.** If the leader has been successful in helping the team prepare for change, then everyone can advance to Goal 2. This goal focuses on two key objectives: spreading the word and planning the change.

First, everyone must get lots of information about the need for change. If the leader doesn't make the case for change, then the old habits will become even more entrenched.

Generally, people use three criteria when deciding whether or not to make a change: relative advantage, compatibility and complexity. Is the new way better than the old way? Does the new way fit into my life, or my job, as I know it? Is the new way easy to understand and use? If the answer is "no" to any of these questions, then resistance to change will spring up.

Jeremy, a participant in one of my recent workshops, gave an excellent example of how these issues were handled really well by his employer in a recent software upgrade. His supervisor pulled together a small group of influential people in his unit and demonstrated the new software, while describing how it was a significant upgrade to the old software. It also made life more convenient and was simple to use and easy to understand. These individuals then spread the word to others, making the change in his company relatively painless.

The second engagement requirement, illustrated by Jeremy's experience, is the need to bring people together to plan the change. How should the change be introduced? How should people be trained? What kind of support will people receive if they have questions? Should it be introduced all at once or in stages?

The team needs to answer these questions in order to increase the chances that others will buy into the change. Having no plan will almost guarantee failure. Jeremy is one of the lucky ones. His boss understood change and introduced it successfully, with the right engagement strategy.

**Goal 3: Rollout.** After giving people a chance to decide to change and plan its adoption, it's time to roll it out in a deliberate and systematic way. People are less resistant to change when they understand it and see the need for it. When the change is rolled out gradually and with the appropriate support and training, its features can be appreciated and its advantages understood by all.

You've probably heard horror stories about companies that have rolled out a change too quickly, without much of a plan. The organization is in chaos. Not enough information or off-target information is provided, causing people to become upset—and often, the company simply stops functioning. Planning the rollout is complex, with many small, important details to be ironed out.

Often the biggest rollout mistakes companies make is lacking the necessary training or demonstration of the new system. Trainers must be experienced at working with diverse kinds of employees, so they can listen to concerns and make themselves available for any questions.

**Goal 4: Confirmation.** A common question that people ask in the midst of change is, "How's it going?" Change brings a great deal of uncertainty. To address the uncertainty, it's important to keep everyone aware of how the change is progressing. People want this kind of confirmation. It must be specific, and it must be truthful.

If Goal 3 is achieved, you'll have the metrics in place for evaluating the change. The key is to keep people informed about the change so it's clear that management is on top of the shift, addressing emerging issues and handling any challenges. How smoothly is the change happening? Today, many companies set up an internal website that contains a dashboard with green, yellow and red lights that indicate whether or not the changes are on track.

## Step 3: Select the right cards

When change shifts from the planning phase to the implementation phase, the Leader Card is really important. People expect the leader to play his or her card when uncertainty is high. They want the leader to make sense out of the chaos. The topics people expect to hear are those explaining the change and the rationale for it. People have to know that the leader is behind the change and knows what he or she is doing.

Team members also want the leader to be visible during the change. The leader should walk around, listen to concerns and provide input when needed. This visibility will calm the waters while also showing a commitment to change.

Another card that employees expect the leader to play is the Team Member Card. Team members support one another, both on job-related issues and personal issues. People must feel that the leader cares about them, as people, and is genuinely interested in getting to know them—at least as a team member, though not necessarily as a friend.

## Step 4: Play to win

The best way to win the Driving-change Game is to create a communication plan that lays out the compelling case for change. An effective plan should connect with key audiences to forge long-lasting business relationships, while keeping everyone informed about the organization's activities. If you have an internal communication team, let them assist—or, at the least, keep them updated about your activities.

Consider these elements when creating your plan:

1. **Target audience analysis.** What are the primary and secondary, internal and external target audiences that need to know about the proposed changes? What levels of knowledge or types of attitudes are these audiences likely

to have about the proposed change? Will any behavioral habits pose an issue?

2. **Situation Analysis.** What internal and external barriers are present that may prevent your message from having the intended impact?

3. **Goals.** What changes in the primary and secondary target audiences—in knowledge levels, attitudes, and behavioral changes—do you want the communication to achieve? Make sure the changes are stated as measurable goals.

4. **Message and media tactics.** What specific message tactics will you implement to overcome key barriers and achieve your goals? What specific communication tactics will you implement to achieve your goals?

5. **Logistics.** Who will administer the communication plan internally? How will audience feedback be processed? Who will serve as communication contacts for the organization? What training will be required to ensure consistency among the communicators?

6. **Evaluation.** What evidence will you gather from the primary and secondary audiences to determine whether or not your message has accomplished its goals? The method should specify when and how the metrics will be collected. To determine message penetration, you might create a short survey to determine who received the message and their takeaway from it.

7. **Budget.** Specify the budget for each communication product and evaluation task. Include a timeline for completing the evaluation.

Thinking about these seven elements and about how to communicate a change, it's important to start at the beginning—with an audience analysis. Don't just start with the message that motivates and makes sense to you. The change is not about you. It's about the *audience*—the people who have to implement the change. What do they think? What do they like?

Usually, there's something really important that determines an audience's interest in change. What would be the biggest factor that the audience values—the most important factor that would

*Identifying that most-important factor, determined in Goal 1, drives the rest of the decision-making.*

turn their opinion positive for the change being advocated? Identifying that most-important factor, determined in Goal 1, drives the rest of the decision-making.

I was once asked by a very traditional church to help its leaders change worship focus from a customary Sunday service to a more evangelical experience that included video and contemporary music. That was a huge change for them. Through research, we discovered that a main factor driving this change was the need to attract more young families. The church was getting too "old."

We asked young families in the church what they wanted, and they responded with a desire for a more contemporary experience. They wanted more energy in the church. The change to a contemporary service became the focus of the communication plan, and after surveying members, we discovered they were all in favor of it. They even suggested two services—a contemporary one, and a more traditional one. It was a win-win.

The point is that failure to consider audience perceptions—understanding their wants, needs and fears—often dooms chances for change. As a leader, it's your job to drive this process and begin in the right place.

# The Negotiation Game

The Negotiation Game is a version of the Problem-solving Game. The goal of the Negotiation Game is to create a solution to a problem that both parties share. And, like most other varieties of the Problem-solving Game, neither party can solve the problem without the other party's participation and eventual consent.

As we know from Chapter 5, what often derails problem-solving is identity attacks, whether inflicted on purpose or by accident. When identity attacks surface, problem-solving turns into conflict, and the goal becomes identity restoration. Once identities have been restored, the parties can get back to problem-solving.

Carrie was a participant in one of my workshops. She was a sales representative from a fast-growing craft beer company. When we started talking about negotiation strategies, she raised her hand to ask a question.

"When I call on alcohol distributors to sell my beer, the first thing they do is try and intimidate me, to get a lower price. They say, 'I'll give you $10 a case for your beer, no more or less, and you have 20 seconds to either take the deal or move on.'

That's really intimidating, and I don't know how to counter that aggressive approach."

I suggested that Carrie shift the game from competitive negotiation to collaborative negotiation with one simple phrase: "Why do you want that?" Asking the "why" question gets beneath the rigid position statement and tries to understand the issue, to move to a more collaborative dialogue. Carrie agreed to try that the next time she made a sales call.

A month later, I ran into Carrie at a local store. She came running up to me and said, "You won't believe what happened!" Her story began with a sales call she had made the day after our workshop. True to form, the guy she called on made the same aggressive demand. "I'll give you $10 a case, take it or leave it." Carrie then tried shifting the Negotiation Game from position-based (focused only on outcome) to issue-based (focusing on key issues to be addressed in advance of solutions). She asked, "Why do you want that?"

The guy gave Carrie a puzzled look and said, "No one has ever asked me that before. Let me think about it, and then I'll tell you the reason."

Carrie said they had a 90-minute conversation about his business, the beers he carried, his marketing challenges and several other important topics. At the end of the conversation he agreed to represent her craft beer line at $20 per case, which was far beyond her expectations. Carrie found that he qualified for a good chunk of marketing money that she could bring to the table, which really helped his business. It developed into a win-win for everyone.

## Step 1: Name the game

Carrie's success story illustrates an important principle of the Negotiation Game: building value for all parties. The key to effective negotiation lies in both parties exchanging proposals and offers to resolve disputed issues, and thus building value for all. It is not about intimidation, bullying the other side or coercion; it's about finding solutions to problems that benefit everyone and cement a productive, long-term relationship.

What is value? Quite simply, it's a ratio of a solution that was selected to solve a specific problem, divided by the cost needed to acquire that solution.

Here is the simple formula:

$$VALUE = \frac{PROBLEM - SOLUTION}{COST}$$

We think a pair of jeans is a great value if they solve a few specific problems: maybe they fit well, last a long time and make us look good. And, as a bonus, they don't cost very much.

We use this same equation every time we judge a product or service. The product or service is a great value if it solves all our problems for a reasonable price. Something is a bad value if it fails to solve the problem, or problems. When that happens, we focus on the price because we feel cheated.

Carrie and her distributor created value in their interaction when Carrie changed the frame and got beyond the distributor's intimidating offer. She shifted it from a position-based negotiation to an issue-based negotiation. They began simply, by talking about their mutual problems, and quickly learned that if they helped each other, both could benefit.

Not only did Carrie change the frame by asking the "why" question, but she also did not fall into the identity trap the distributor tried to shove her into. He began by attacking her positive and negative face. He treated Carrie disrespectfully by throwing out a very intimidating, unfriendly, high-power, lowball offer. He was very rude. That threatened her positive face, or her desire to be seen as a competent professional. Then he forced her to make a very quick decision. He threatened her negative face by trying to push her around.

These two identity threats would normally redefine a negotiation as the Conflict Game, in which people would exchange face attacks while also trying to defend their identities against such attacks. Not much substantive interaction occurs in the Conflict Game. As we know, that game is focused on identity restoration.

By ignoring the attacks and shifting the frame, Carrie refused to play the Conflict Game and continued to play the Problem-solving Game. She kept the discussion focused on mutual business interests. That was well done, and it paid off for both parties.

## Step 2: Have simple goals

The main reason for relaying Carrie's story is to point out that the simple goal of all negotiations should be a focus on **creating value**—trying to learn about one another's key problems and then creatively addressing those problems. Once that value has been created, then the parties can focus on **claiming value**—taking their share of the expanded pie.

Of course, many people don't care about creating value. They instead want to claim whatever value they may have as quickly as possible. Common wisdom seems to be that negotiations should be adversarial: It's all about intimidating the opponent, in order to walk all over them.

Research is very clear that this strategy simply does not work, either in the short term or in the long term. What ends up happening is that people act aggressively toward one another, attacking identities right and left. The Conflict Game makes it difficult to focus on creative problem-solving. Parties end up dis-advantaging themselves, rather than gaining a real advantage.

## Step 3: Select the right cards

The Negotiator Card is very similar to the Leader Card in the sense that both cards require taking charge of the decision-making process. The negotiation process is described below, and it's useful to follow this general guideline in order to manage the topics and issues that emerge in negotiation.

Negotiators need to hold other talk cards, as well. To build an effective relationship with the different parties, the negotiator might need the Acquaintance Card, which allows for personal topics to be exchanged. Displaying a sense of humor might occasionally be useful, calling for the Comedian Card. The Expert Card will also be required, as negotiators need to provide substantive information during the interaction.

In addition to being concerned with the topics on these various cards, negotiators must pay special attention to style choices—and for several reasons. Of most importance is that the negotiator avoids choosing styles that might offend the other party's positive or negative face. For example, constantly using high-power and unfriendly styles could be viewed as confrontational. As we know, when both parties start down this path, they begin playing the Conflict Game and focus on identity management rather than substantive issues.

To avoid these kinds of issues, negotiators need to be aware of their communication style preferences. Based on your communication style preferences, are you, as a negotiator, more focused on the topics in play or the relationship issues that crop up during the interaction? Effective negotiators need to create a productive working relationship while paying attention to the substantive details of the settlement agreement.

## Step 4: Play to win

If you scored well on the Communication Style Inventory in Chapter 3, then you are confident in confronting problems constructively. Maybe the best way to bolster your confidence is to describe the four stages of negotiation that will help you create value and win the Negotiation Game for both parties. Let's take a look at these four stages, and see what the process looks like.

**Stage 1: Build the relationships.** Any effective problem-solving activity begins with the parties simply getting to know one another. The goal is to build understanding and basic interpersonal trust. Parties probably play the Acquaintance Card, or even the Friend Card, and share general information. They could also play the Colleague Card, or other professional cards, as long as they begin by understanding the general situation they find themselves in at that point. Hopefully, parties can learn to open lines of communication and create a sense of mutual respect, so they are less vulnerable to the risk of offending one another and moving into the Conflict Game.

When Carrie called on her client, she really did not have a chance to build a relationship in a casual, friendly way. The client was immediately confrontational. Only when Carrie changed the frame by asking the "why" question did the general sharing of information begin. The client opened up, and relationship building began—with a general discussion about both Carrie's and the client's businesses.

**Stage 2: Understand the issues.** At some point in this discussion, parties will transition to the issues they want to discuss. It's best not to start this discussion with fixed positions—that's very adversarial. It encourages people to dig in their heels and defend their identities, which takes them into the Conflict Game.

The best way to begin is to identify the full range of issues each person would like to discuss. I hope it's clear at this point that there are always two sets of issues: **identity** and **material**.

Recall that identity issues are about positive and negative face. People are always sensitive to these issues, talking about such things as fairness, trust, respect or being listened to. When you hear these words, particularly over and over again, then the person is moving into the Conflict Game and trying to acknowledge that their identity is being challenged.

Material issues are about the substantive matters of the negotiation, such as money, goods and services. For Carrie and her customer, these issues focused on things like price per case, marketing strategies, delivery schedules and the like. It's always important to identify the range of issues first, before making proposals about each of them separately.

**Stage 3: Bundle the issues.** The reason it's important to discover the full range of material issues is that identifying them up front allows you to create value by bundling them into one package. Often, negotiators' interests in these issues are very different. Carrie was interested in price per case while her client was interested in receiving marketing money that could spread across his entire product line. To her client, Carrie's craft beers represented a small fraction of his business, yet the marketing money she provided could be leveraged more broadly. Together, they created value. He paid her the price per case she needed, and she gave him the marketing money he hadn't expected, but wanted.

Even identity issues can fall into the bundle, if needed. Recall the incident with the woman contemplating suicide by jumping off the bridge. The police negotiator learned that the woman's husband had cheated on her and that she no longer wanted to live. This is an extreme identity issue: she was no longer able to play the Wife Card.

The hostage negotiator wanted to add material issues to balance this loss of identity. He started talking about her daughters and the need for her to be there to raise them. That conversation created value by, once again, shifting the frame. He encouraged the woman to view the issue from her children's perspective and not her own.

Unfortunately, negotiators often fall into the trap of negotiating issues separately. This approach creates unnecessary competition between the parties and stirs up identity issues. When people look at one issue at a time, it's strictly a win-lose situation. The more one person gets on that one issue, the less the other person gets. Bundling a range of issues allows for tradeoffs and other means of coming up with a package deal that's best for everyone. Again, it's all about building value.

**Stage 4: Finalize the deal.** Once value has been created, it can be claimed. Parties can take their portion of a bigger pie. Negotiators need to be clear about what, when and how they claim their rewards. Finalizing the deal means identifying the specific details that must be ironed out and agreed upon. Perhaps the contract needs to be signed and other details arranged.

*Bundling a range of issues allows for tradeoffs and other means of coming up with a package deal that's best for everyone.*

When Carrie ended the negotiation with her new customer, she was very clear about the final arrangement. She first outlined what they agreed upon. Next, she laid out a timeline for when and how those details would be executed. The craft beer would be delivered by a specific date, the marketing money would be distributed in a particular sequence, etc.

The point is, *don't rush*! Take your time in making sure that every detail is covered so there are no surprises later on. Less ambiguity in the final arrangement is best.

The end of the Negotiation Game doesn't really happen when the negotiation is over. Business relationships are always in play and perpetually in motion. Delivering on promises and following through with every detail builds trust and makes subsequent negotiations much easier.

## Positive and Negative Framing Bias

While these four stages look fairly straightforward, there are several biases negotiators bring to the table that can make it difficult to create value. We have already examined the single-issue biases that many negotiators have. One of the well-researched biases focuses on the frames that people have when entering the Negotiation Game.

What are the frames, and how do they impact the negotiations?

**Negative frames:** The Problem-solving Game is more likely to become the Conflict Game, focusing on identity issues, when the parties approach the interaction using a negative frame bias. A negative frame bias is an attitude that says, "I want to protect what I have at all costs; I want to do what it takes to win the game and prove that I am right and can't be pushed around."

The negative frame bias is not about standing up for your rights, which is certainly appropriate. It's about trying to defeat the other person as a means of saving face or looking tough. Carrie's new customer is a classic example of a negative frame bias. He likes to look tough and intimidate people. It's his way of extorting money from suppliers. In reality, the negative frame bias focuses on identity issues first, and material issues second.

**Positive frames:** A positive frame takes the opposite approach: Where a negative frame focuses on restoring personal identities, a positive frame focuses on material opportunities. It says, "Hey, I'm focused on what I can gain from the situation and I look ahead to a better future, rather than trying to protect the past by bullying my opponent." Carrie successfully changed her client's frame from negative to positive by asking the "why" question.

In reality, negative frames are about looking backward to achieve justice, fairness and identity restoration. Positive frames are about looking forward to achieve gains in material issues. Negative frames move people away from the Problem-solving Game and into the Conflict Game—and then they keep them there, which allows conflict to escalate. Positive frames keep people in the Problem-solving Game. As we know, people will occasionally slip into the Conflict Game when their negative frame and identity-restoration biases flare up. The goal is to shift the frame and spend most of the time problem-solving.

# Transforming Conflict Into Problem-solving Through Relationship Development

One line of thinking among negotiation practitioners believes that material issues in conflicts are best resolved when parties first learn to transform their relationship. The thinking holds that parties that don't like or trust one another are more likely to violate one another's identities, casting them frequently into the Conflict Game. Starting the negotiation by building the relationship prevents this problem.

Recall that Stage 1 in the Negotiation Game is about building the relationship. The question lies in how to specifically approach this problem. The first task in reforming the relationship is to build **recognition**. Parties must be able to recognize the full impact of the conflict on one another, both materially and emotionally. This recognition pulls the focus away from the individual's own identity restoration needs and instead looks at what the other person is experiencing.

This recognition changes the frame from negative to positive—from looking backward, to achieve identity restoration, to looking forward, to collaborate and build value. The process of collaboration involves each person recognizing the other's identity and material goals, and helping them work toward achieving them. This recognition is often very powerful in shifting back into the Problem-solving Game.

Do you recall the mediation case described in Chapter 4, between Beth and Ann? Beth accused Ann of vandalizing her car. Ann denied it. They argued back and forth for a while.

The mediator then remarked that the two women seemed to know one another. They both admitted that they used to be best friends. One of the women revealed that the friendship ended when the other woman had an affair with her boyfriend. The jilted woman then admitted to vandalizing the other's car. They both started crying, indicating that the man was an idiot whom both had abandoned long ago and that they missed each other.

After seeing that the relationship had been restored, the mediator moved on to the vandalism issue. The woman who admitted to vandalizing the car quickly agreed to pay for any damages. In other words, the relationship transformation moved them from the Conflict Game into the Problem-solving Game.

The second element of constructive conflict is **empowerment.** When we are empowered, we have the skill and courage to take on identity and material issues. Do parties feel they can discuss their issues and stick with the discussion, to resolve and possibly transform the conflict? Some key communication skills necessary for effective card talk games are:

- Listening to the other's position
- Speaking respectfully by talking about views on issues while keeping away from personal attacks
- Being able to generate creative solutions to both parties' problems
- Working through a specific process for structuring the discussion, so it does not get off track

This process of integration, or coming together, is about identifying issues and generating options to address them. Don't become concerned if you are beginning the Negotiation Game and you are focusing on differences; that's to be expected. But once those differences have emerged, the issue is this: How can you integrate your interests and come up with creative solutions to build value that *both of you* can use to create positive change?

Remember, effective negotiation is all about building value. Value is determined by evaluating how well problems were solved in relation to the cost of achieving the solution. If both parties were happy about how they jointly solved a problem, and hassles were minimal, then they created value. Building value takes a commitment to spend the time necessary to create these win-win solutions.

To help you plan your next negotiation, here is a planning tool you might find helpful:

## The Negotiation Planner

## The issues:

- What are the top three issues or problems you must solve in this negotiation? Describe each issue or problem in a few words:

- Which of these three issues is your top priority?

- What are the top three issues that the other negotiator is concerned about? Describe them in a few words:

- Which of these three issues is their top priority, in your view?

## The communication strategies:

- What kind of relational messages do you want to send? Formal or informal? Friendly or distant? In control or one-down?

- What topics can you discuss to support the other party's identity?

## Proposal development:

- Can you combine the issues into one proposal?

- Can you create a new approach to solve the problem?

## Offers:

- What will be your opening offer?

- What issue is likely to be your first concession?

## Information sharing:

- What information about your issues are you willing to share first?

- What other key points of information are you willing to share?

## Information seeking:

- What are two or three key questions you need to ask the other party?

- What listening strategies will be most effective?

# The Performance Appraisal Game

As we move through these chapters, notice that the talk card games become more at risk for turning into the Conflict Game. A really difficult critical conversation that many leaders avoid is the Employee Evaluation Meeting Game, or the Performance Appraisal Game. You know the drill: The interview is scheduled, and both the boss and the employee dread the conversation.

## Step 1: Name the game

Consider Alexis, the sales manager of a large metropolitan media company. She is constantly overwhelmed, working with staff to drive sales. In the midst of all this, she gets an email from human resources indicating that she has not completed her employee evaluation forms for last year.

After cursing the email and saying to herself that evaluations are a waste of time, Alexis went to the company's evaluation web page and completed a form for each sales-person, giving every-one the maximum rating in each area. After all, she thought, ratings don't really matter—only sales numbers matter.

This is not an atypical reaction to employee evaluations. Many managers believe that evaluations are a waste of time and have little impact on the company's overall performance. They are simply a formality. But they're wrong! The Performance Appraisal Game is critically important for the employee, the manager and the organization. Talent is every organization's No. 1 resource, and developing that talent should be a top priority for any leader.

Research tells us that there are many reasons why performance appraisals may be *the* most important driver of a company's success. These appraisals not only shape the direction of the employee's performance; they clarify and solidify the performance standards of the company. If they are not taken seriously, then the organization is not serious about performance. It's that simple.

It's not fair to blame Alexis for her failure to take the evaluations seriously. She is probably responding to the norm for her company. It's likely that no one at her company takes evaluations seriously, and it is certainly not driven by top leadership—or it would have been a priority that was talked about, trained on and followed up with.

The point is that, despite the apprehension, the company and each if its leaders should get behind this critical conversation and take full advantage of it. To help you feel more comfortable having an effective performance appraisal interview with a team member, let's answer some important questions about that task.

## Why Are Performance Appraisal Interviews Important?

For many years, scholars in the area of performance appraisal have conducted studies to understand their impact. It turns out that there are lots of positives that derive from effective performance appraisal interviews. Here are several of them, so you can get a rich understanding of the role they serve in successful organizations:

- **It's all about the system.** In other words, it's not just about the interviews themselves. An evaluation system with many different components needs to be in place. A complete system may include a written policy that outlines performance standards, rating categories and the frequency of ratings. If you can't recall where the system is identified and what the system consists of, then either you don't have one or you haven't been trained on it.

- **Performance objectives or standards let everyone see clearly what it takes to succeed in the unit and in the organization.** When employees know how high the bar is—and the importance of getting over the bar is constantly reinforced—they are more likely to get over the bar. That just makes sense. Most people want to succeed and want to clear goal posts. When they can see the bar, and know it is highly valued by upper management, they know where to aim.

- **An effective performance appraisal system strengthens employee perceptions of social justice.** The perception of social justice relates to the idea of whether or not the company is fair and just in dealing with people. It speaks to the identity issue of respect. A company that is just and fair is respectful of employees. The company demonstrates a commitment to basic human dignity by showing that the rules are the same for everyone. There are no special deals; no one is discriminated against based on a secret score card.

- **During times of rapid change in the company, effective systems help people believe in the stability of the organization.** Research reveals that effective systems help people better adapt to change because the rules for what counts as performance are stable. It's an anchor that people can hold on to. And, the size of this anchor is pretty substantial. When people understand and have confidence in the performance appraisal system, they view the organization as a whole as much more stable.

That's important in persuading people to make a long-term commitment to the company and reducing turnover. While the way of doing business might change regularly, the company as a whole needs to be viewed as stable. Performance appraisal systems are one way to achieve this.

- **Performance appraisal systems improve the relationship between employer and employee, even when employee ratings are poor.** Yes, even when the employee is rated poorly for performance, the Performance Appraisal Game can improve the employee-employer relationship. That's because if the system is fair and just, then the employer or manager will also be seen as fair and just by the employee. That increases trust and allows for more open communication between parties.

# What Are the Benefits of a Well-designed and Properly Executed Performance Management System?

- **For employees:** A well-designed system improves self-esteem by providing a clear path forward to improve performance skills. Employees feel much better about their career when the path forward is less ambiguous. When performance standards are unclear, and the ability to get feedback is limited, uncertainty kicks in. Not knowing what to do or what's valued is paralyzing for most people.

- **For managers:** A well-designed system is invaluable on many fronts. First, a system that is well understood increases employee motivation, since standards—and instructions for how to achieve those standards—are clear. Effective interviews provide better insight into employee circumstances: life situations, interests and skill sets. That insight leads to increased employee competence and motivation, as well as enhanced communication about employee performance.

- **For companies:** The benefits of a well-designed system are very empowering. The system provides clear goals so that everyone can understand what's valued. Research also reveals that a well-understood system reduces misconduct while providing better protection against lawsuits. Clear performance appraisal systems that include specific company goals also help staff understand the company's vision and mission. In other words, everyone understands how the change fits in with what the company is trying to achieve, thereby making each employee's role more comprehensible.

## Step 2: Have simple goals

The simple goal of the Performance Appraisal Game is employee development. It's all about having a conversation that aligns organizational expectations with employee expectations. Think about your best and worst performance appraisal interview, as a team member. What separates them? What did you like about the best interview, and why was the worst interview such a problem?

You probably remember the bad one much more clearly than the good one. Negative experiences leave a lasting impression on people. The point is to not let these experiences prevent you from playing the Performance Appraisal Game effectively.

We know from research that performance appraisals go much more smoothly if some best practices are followed:

- **Performance standards and data collection techniques should be transparent and well understood by each employee from the day he or she gets hired.** Imagine hiring into a company where performance standards are not well understood. Your boss just told you to work hard, and that everything will take care of itself. Under these conditions it's tough to know when you're doing well and when you're doing poorly. This kind of ambiguity can lead to confusion about how an individual fits into an organization, which creates many identity challenges for employees, as we discussed in Chapter 4.

- **The appraisal process should include a self-evaluation that each team member writes up prior to the meeting.** What is the team member's assessment of his or her own performance on each standard? The specific, objective data associated with each person's performance should be well known by the time the evaluation meeting is held. For employees, it's important to capture their open-ended thoughts about their performance. What did they think they did well? What areas need development? What could help them improve? What resources are needed to enhance productivity? What barriers need to be removed?

- **The structure of the interview, or evaluation, should be understood in advance and taken seriously by both the leader and the team member.** The evaluation should be perceived as structured, substantive and constructive. In other words, everyone knows what to expect in terms of both substance and time. The goal is to make sure that everyone has a chance to drill down into the issues and then come out of the session with a clear understanding of how to move forward. A lack of structure increases ambiguity, which is not productive.

- **The goal of the interview should always be team member development: achieving personal and professional goals.** What are the members' goals, and are they on track to achieve them? When a person is hired into the organization, the question is always, "Is this person a good fit?" The ongoing objective of any evaluation system is to help that person be an even better fit, going forward. Ideally, the organization should help shape each employee, as the employees also help shape the organization into an even better place. Employee development is the way to think about the goal of this critical conversation.

- **The team member should receive a written evaluation soon after the meeting that provides a clear sense of where he or she stands in the unit and what resources are needed to help him or her perform even better.** "Personal development plan" is a good name for the specific document that the employee should have after leaving the interview. Right there, in black and white, the employee can see what's needed to grow. Receiving the employer's evaluation before coming to the meeting is important, as well, so there are no surprises.

## Step 3: Select the right cards

The performance appraisal critical conversation must be played with cards that allow the employee to open up and have a productive, friendly exchange. Just like the challenge in playing the Negotiator Card, the Employer/Manager Card needs to be sensitive to both the topics and style choices of the appraisal process. Remember, identities are at risk here. Whenever anyone is being evaluated, it is a threat to positive face. We all want to look competent and effective, but negative feedback is unavoidable; everyone can't be good at everything! We all have room for improvement.

In particular, the interviewer should be sensitive to playing cards capable of putting the interviewee at ease. Perhaps the Acquaintance Card, Friend Card or Mentor Card, played at different points, can show empathy and concern. The point is to not stick with one card and hope that card carries the day. Be ready with multiple professional cards and multiple personal cards.

## Step 4: Play to win

How is the Performance Appraisal Game played so that all parties have a productive, positive experience? Here are some best practices for how to play this important game:

1. **Create a structure for the interview.** Each interview should have a specific beginning, middle and end. Start by asking the employee what is working and allow the employee to lead.

    The beginning should be a relationship-builder and very open-ended, with the goal of having the employee doing most of the talking. Pay close attention. For some staff, it may be the only time of the year they disclose hurdles that hinder their progress.

    The middle should go over each performance area. The goal is to review the performance metrics so that each party understands them and has some context for what they really mean.

    The end should be committed to creating a plan for the future. What needs to be developed, and what resources are needed to get there?

1. **Provide feedback based on strengths, not weaknesses.** Don't abandon a discussion of weaknesses, but instead focus on an employee's knowledge and skills in *overcoming* weaknesses. Don't focus on talents, either: Knowledge and skills can be learned and changed, whereas talents are more individual-specific and ambiguous.

2. **Be considerate.** Provide at least three positives for every negative, since people overweigh negatives. It's only natural to overreact to negative feedback: When a goal is not met, it's a threat to one's positive face, or identity. We all want to be blemish-free in our public image.

3. **Ensure familiarity.** Sometimes, evaluations are done by an outsider—say, someone from human resources, who has no familiarity with the employee. This is a huge mistake. The evaluation is only perceived as honest and

*When follow-up critical conversations happen, the employee understands that the real goal is success in the job and making sure that everything is coming together.*

fair when it is conducted by the immediate supervisor. That person knows the employee's history and sees the individual on a regular basis. Without that relationship, an evaluation has little credibility. Remember, when evaluations are done well, they actually enhance the relationship between the employee and the supervisor.

4. **Deliver feedback in a private, confidential setting.** The actual critical conversation should be done in a private setting, with plenty of time allocated for the discussion. This gives both parties the opportunity to play multiple talk cards during the interaction, as they learn to relate to each other on multiple levels. Public criticism only weakens the trust between employer and employee. Discussions must be confidential so that people can open up and express emotions if necessary.

5. **Provide feedback that is specific and accurate, and tied to the unit and the organization.** Focusing on skills and competencies, rather than on talents or more ambiguous issues, is most productive. The more specific, the better, in terms of both what needs to be corrected and what's working well.

6. **Follow up.** End with a plan for the year ahead and agree to periodic checkups associated with the plan. Failure to check up means that the plan is not real, or not important. When follow-up critical conversations happen, the employee understands that the real goal is success in the job and making sure that everything is coming together.

# What Are Common Interview Mistakes?

What are some common mistakes that leaders make when conducting performance appraisals? Think about our friend Alexis. The biggest mistake she made was not taking the appraisal process seriously. As mentioned earlier, perhaps these appraisals were not taken seriously within the organization, as was evidenced by Alexis's boss not holding her accountable for blowing off the performance appraisals.

**Mistake 1: Not taking them seriously.** It's probably a good thing that Alexis did not conduct appraisal interviews with her sales team members, because she probably would not have taken them seriously nor done a good job. Research tells us that when a performance appraisal is done poorly, it can cause more harm than good. That is, a bad interview can erode trust in the supervisor and faith in the organization. "They don't care, why should I?" might be the response.

**Mistake 2: Being too quick.** A second common mistake is conducting the appraisal interviews too quickly. Not taking sufficient time to work through all areas of performance risks doing a bad job. There is a beginning, a middle and an end, as well as a structure that must be followed for each interview. It takes time to drill down into issues and really understand what's in play regarding someone's performance. Life is complicated and everyone has a story that's important. You would not want your doctor to rush through a conversation regarding your health. Think of time as the first step toward quality.

**Mistake 3: Getting too specific too quickly.** The beginning of the interview should be very open-ended and focused on relationship building. "How's it going?" or "What are you excited about?" might be some icebreakers that just start a general discussion about the person's professional development. This casual conversation gives the employee the chance to surface concerns. Getting too specific too quickly usually takes the form of asking closed-ended questions to begin the session. This pattern discourages open communication. Beginning with open-ended questions is more of an employee-centered approach and is more open and considerate.

**Mistake 4: Thinking about appraisals as a chore.** A common mistake, certainly made by Alexis, is not viewing appraisal interviews as a developmental opportunity. Alexis saw them as a chore. My question to her would be, "Then how do you shape the professional development of your sales team members?" Many leaders think they can just walk around, talk to the staff and manage in a minute! Sure, walking around can be useful, but it's not all that's needed. Taking time to have critical conversations within the structure of an appraisal interview is essential.

**Mistake 5: Having no clear improvement plan.** Leaving the performance appraisal without a clear plan for moving forward can happen when the process is rushed. What should the person continue to do? What new direction might the person pursue? What resources will be available to make all of this work?

# The Performance Appraisal Game as a Leadership Imperative

It should be apparent by now that anyone playing the Leader Card should have, in their arsenal, expertise in conducting an effective performance appraisal interview. Do you recall the five leadership expectations, discussed in Chapter 4, that employees have when someone plays the Leader Card? Two key dimensions were **enabling others to act** and **encouraging the heart**.

Alexis punted the opportunity to fulfill both of these key leader-ship obligations by skirting her duties to conduct performance appraisals.

Think about it: When are employees entitled to receiving strong direction that empowers them to perform well? Always, right? If the leader thinks that having a one-minute conversation can pull it all together to set a clear, empowering direction for an employee, it's a big mistake.

Performance appraisals are milestones for both leaders and team members. The research could not be clearer on this point. These are critical conversations that are pivotal in one's career. And they are pivotal for stocking the company with great employees. As a result, they should happen in a structured, empowering way that provides clear direction.

That's what leadership does. It shapes. It organizes. It moti-vates. Performance appraisals are a chance to establish clear and decisive leadership. Don't pass up this opportunity.

# The Presenting Game

Perhaps the biggest mistake people make when giving PowerPoint presentations is drilling the audience with boring facts. "Death by PowerPoint" is a common expression, and it refers to people being bored to death by one PowerPoint slide after another. Presentations should be interactive: they should form the basis for a productive conversation. They should *not* be viewed as a survival task.

Travis was a student in one of my communication graduate courses. He recalled an incident with his commanding officer (Travis was in the military) in which the officer's presentation was incredibly irrelevant, boring and non-interactive. At the end of the PowerPoint presentation, the officer asked if there were any questions—and of course, there were only crickets—stone silence.

Finally, Travis felt sorry for the officer and decided to say something just to rescue his presentation. A brief discussion ensued that allowed people to leave on a better-informed and positive note. Later, the officer thanked Travis for stimulating some conversation.

Then he asked Travis, "Why didn't others speak up?" Travis replied, "Because you were only playing the Commanding

*Perhaps the biggest mistake that people make when giving PowerPoint (PP) presentations is drilling the audience with boring facts.*

Officer Card and nothing else. When you play that card, you ask everyone else to play the passive Soldier Card, which discourages them from 'questioning' you." Travis suggested that the officer lighten up the presentation with some humor (the Comedian Card) and perhaps some personal references (the Friend Card). He might also try the Colleague Card, and give the group a team task before asking for input on the problem.

## Step 1: Name the game

Make no mistake—the Presenting Game is a critical conversation, and should be approached from this perspective. After all, the purpose of most professional PowerPoint presentation is problem-solving. You have an issue that you would like to bring before the team, and you use PowerPoint to generate a discussion about some solutions. Think of it first as a tool to enhance and clarify a critical conversation. The question is, what are the rules for structuring the Presenting Game in order to achieve this goal?

# Five Rules for Structuring the Presenting Game

**Rule 1: Make a point.** The last thing you want to see after a presentation is people walking away confused about what you said. There has to be a main point, and you should be able to say the point in less than 10 words. You want to make the point near the beginning, reinforce it during the presentation, and then make it again at the end so people remember it.

Of course, if the presentation is boring or extremely technical, you could still state the point and no one would get it because they all tuned out. I can't tell you how many presentations I have come away from confused about what the presenter was really trying to say. And, most of the time, I was paying attention!

**Rule 2: Tell a story.** Think of your presentation as a series of stories. Stories make messages memorable. They have a beginning, middle and end. They make a point. The bottom line: Stories help people learn. In fact, you relive your most memorable moments as stories that you tell others.

The most important story you want to tell is the point of the presentation itself. In essence, the whole presentation is a story. There's a problem that needs to be solved; here are the options and methods for solving the problem, and here's the best solution—beginning, middle and end. Think about your presentation as telling a story.

A great way to introduce stories in your presentation is at the beginning, as an attention-getter. It is very effective to begin your presentation by telling a story about the impact of the problem on someone's personal situation.

I recently gave a presentation about critical conversations to a group of media executives. I began with a hostage negotiation story that showed the importance of building a personal relationship through casual conversation. The story had a huge influence on the ability of the audience to remember the point I was trying to make: the value of casual conversation.

**Rule 3: Make it interactive.** Presentations should be interactive. They should be a critical conversation. How many times have you sat through boring PowerPoint presentations and looked at your phone or computer so you could do "real" work? People tune out if the session is not a conversation.

So how can you make a presentation a conversation? The key is playing multiple cards with varying styles. Sure, the main card you'll probably play is the Expert Card. You have an important message for people about a critical problem that needs to be solved. If you play only that card, though, and lecture to people, you are asking them to play the passive Learner Card and just absorb the information. That's when people begin to tune out.

To get interactive, flip the model. Ask the audience to be the expert and start a conversation about some issue. Write down their thoughts on a flip chart and post the thoughts around the room. It can also be useful to play the Colleague Card, which asks the audience to also play the Colleague Card. This often stimulates a conversation. The point is to *never* play just one card. Play at least three cards during a presentation to make it interactive.

**Rule 4: Make it fun.** Fun presentations are interactive—not cute and entertaining, with jokes and emoji on the screen. "Fun" means that the presentation is emotionally engaging. It means you are willing to be interesting and thoughtful.

One way to achieve a fun presentation is to have an engaging attention-grabber at the beginning of the presentation. I have already talked about the personal-story form of an attention-getter. Another fun, engaging idea is a video that gets people thinking. A 30- to 60-second video that illustrates a key point can be very memorable. But don't force the video to stand on its own. Use it to get people talking and interacting. You might even make it controversial, to stimulate conversation.

Being fun is also important during other parts of the presentation. In the middle, stories are often welcome to keep engagement high. But it's really important to be fun at the end. Certainly, you must tell your audience your main point once again. Attach that main point to a story, or even a funny tale, that really brings it home. Don't be afraid of being engaging. It can make your presentation a wild success!

**Rule 5: Make it clear and compelling.** Finally, we know from the persuasion literature that effective messages are clear, articulate a simple opening thesis and are easily understood. People like organized presentations right from the opening. They want to know where you're going, where you've been and what point you're trying to make. Don't make listening a difficult task for people; make it easy.

Maybe you've been to presentations where the point the presenter is trying to make is unclear. Perhaps the reasoning behind the proposals is fuzzy. If you're playing the Expert Card, the audience will expect an expert presentation, full of supporting ideas and well-reasoned arguments. These kinds of presentations build your credibility and are easy for audience members to accept.

## Presentation Self-Assessment

Critique your last PowerPoint presentation. Go through this checklist to get a sense of how you might have made your PowerPoint better. Take a look at each rule and score yourself on a scale of 0 to 5, with 0 indicating that you did not follow the rule and 5 meaning you did follow the rule. In the Thoughts column, indicate how you either did or did not follow the rules. Be specific.

| Rules | Score | Thoughts |
|---|---|---|
| **Make a Point** | | |
| **Tell a Story** | | |
| **Make it Interactive** | | |
| **Make it Fun** | | |
| **Make it Clear** | | |

If you scored below 15 on this self-assessment, you would benefit from revisiting the rules and asking for feedback on your presentations. It's understandable that people fall into a rut on giving presentations. They play the Expert Card and just start lecturing—that's the easiest thing to do. Such a speaker asks the audience to play the passive Learner Card. Yet this gives the audience a free ticket to ignore the presentation and do something else. Remember, presentations are critical conversations and excellent opportunities to assert leadership.

## Step 2: Have simple goals

The five presentation rules just outlined make it clear that presentations should not try to do too much. A presentation should be a critical conversation about one important point—a thesis statement of some kind. Everything else should revolve around that central point—the stories, the supporting evidence, etc.

Earl is a physician who specializes in emergency medicine. He is known for his ability to diagnose and treat various rare diseases. One afternoon I met with him to go over a project we were working on. When I first came into his office, he was reviewing his PowerPoint slides for a professional presentation. Before our meeting began he showed me his slides. After reviewing a few, I asked how many slides he was going to present—and he responded that he had 88 slides for his 30-minute presentation.

I was aghast. I asked how he could have so many slides. Shouldn't he present just a few slides to tell his story? Earl said he typically does this. He has a very simple story to tell about a specific disease that presents in a very complicated way. He needs to have many pictures, but hardly any verbiage, to run through the various ways the disease can impact patients.

In other words, Earl had a story to tell about a tricky disease. His goal was simple: Help other physicians understand how this disease presents so they can spot it quickly in the emergency room. In this case, 88 slides may work. For everyone else, aim for one slide for every three to five minutes.

## Step 3: Select the right cards

During his presentations, Earl likes to play many cards. Of course he plays the Physician Card and the Expert Card when describing the diseases he is presenting on. Earl also plays the Colleague Card, talking about the challenges associated with diagnosing these issues. He also plays some personal cards to soften up the presentation and make it more relatable.

A presentation is a critical conversation in the sense that it is an invitation to converse about a topic. It is a problem-solving interaction as the PowerPoint explores a specific problem from a particular perspective and invites the audience to contribute.

As a result, the topics and styles that accompany card choices must invite people into the conversation. The Physician Card and the Expert Card are generally not very inviting: they are often played with very formal and high-power styles and encourage a more passive response from an audience. The Colleague Card, or a personal card of some sort, might be perceived as more inviting in terms of audience members contributing.

The point is this: A presenter needs to think carefully about which cards will get the best response from the audience. What will get them talking? As we know from prior chapters, playing just one card is counterproductive. The Presenting Game requires several cards in order to generate a robust critical conversation about the topic.

## Step 4: Play to win

Earl wins most of his PowerPoint critical conversations. His slides generate a great deal of interaction among audience members. Earl's audiences are eager to understand complex disease presentations so that they don't misdiagnose a patient's condition. PowerPoint presentations that lose are ones that anesthetize an audience and put them to sleep. Or worse, they anger an audience for wasting time.

The first step in winning a PowerPoint critical conversation is analyzing the audience. What stories are they interested in hearing? How much detail is needed? How important to them is the point you want to make? What kinds of cards would they find appropriate or inappropriate?

The second step in winning is making sure that the slides are engaging. That typically means few words and several pictures. The real purpose of the slides is to add interest or emotional engagement to the presentation. The *presenter* should tell the story, and not the slides.

Engaging slides also means that the presenter does not simply read slides to an audience. This really turns off an audience. Plus, research shows that audience members can read faster than you can talk. They want an interesting story with engaging slides that makes a specific point.

The third step in winning is to make sure the PowerPoint presentation has an engaging attention-getter on the front end and a captivating conclusion on the back end. The attention-getter must pull the audience into the presenter. It might begin with a personal story that allows the presenter to play a personal card of some sort.

Earl starts his presentations with some slides of the disease he is talking about and then asks the audience to guess what the disease might be and why. It gets people talking quickly.

The ending is even more important. Can you summarize your presentation in an interesting way that leaves the audience motivated to look more into your subject matter and ask questions? The presentation must be remembered with something important, and the final 30 seconds or so is your chance to do that. Earl likes to finish with a personal success story, usually involving a patient with the disease whom he treated and whom is now doing well.

The final step in winning the Presenting Game is making sure that you, as the presenter, are communicating clearly with the audience. That means you are maintaining eye contact with specific individuals in the audience as you move around the room—not standing behind the podium, hiding from the audience. Your voice should carry, so everyone can hear you. You ask questions and invite comments as you present.

Remember, you're playing multiple cards as you have critical conversations with the audience about your presentation topic. Your primary objective is to convince the audience that you, as the speaker, really care about your message—and that you genuinely want the audience to understand your message. If the audience gets the slightest hint that you're up there presenting just to get through it, they will immediately turn off to your message. *Convince them that you care!*

# The Vision Game

Followers expect leaders to build and present a vision of the future. This expectation really comes down to answering three important questions:

1. Where is the organization going?
2. Why are we going there?
3. How do we get there?

Can you answer these questions for your unit, group or business?

History is filled with leaders who asked and answered these three questions. Henry Ford had a vision of mobilizing America: putting America on wheels. He invented the assembly line to make that happen. President Kennedy cast a vision of putting a man on the moon before the end of the 1960s. Then he put resources in place to make that happen. Larry Page and Sergey Brin had a vision to organize the world's information and make it quickly and easily accessible to everyone. They created Google to execute it.

## Step 1: Name the game

These three visions—the visions of Henry Ford, President Kennedy, and Larry Page and Sergey Brin—are simple to understand and explain to others. How might you establish a vision for your slice of the world that is compelling, yet also easy to understand? Consider the case of Shannon, the director of communications and branding at a midsize insurance company, who decided to create a radically different vision for her division that transformed her company.

When Shannon was first hired, she took over the duties of populating the company's social media output. She did a very good job of building the company's presence in this important communication medium, yet she felt that her work was not integrated with the other communications and branding functions in her division.

After about two years of working with social media output, she became convinced that the company was relying on the old "push" method of communication with customers. Instead of engaging customers and listening to their messages, the company fell into the rut of "pushing" its messages out to customers, to establish the brand *they* wanted. Yes, the company was bumping along well financially, but the brand was getting stale and more out of touch with millennials and other key target customers.

After going to a workshop on customer engagement, Shannon understood the need to completely transform the communications and branding division using a customer engagement model that *pulls* people into the brand, rather than pushing endless, delete-able streams of information at them with no significant impact. After getting really fired up about this customer engagement focus, she pitched it to her vice president, who showed little interest.

Then, at an informal company get-together, Shannon ran into the CEO, who asked what she was working on. He loved the customer engagement idea. That brief introduction caught his attention, and he met with Shannon to learn more about it.

A few months later, due to her vice president accepting another position, Shannon interviewed for the position of vice president of corporate communication—and got it.

Her first act was to talk with others in the division about a new focus on customer engagement. They developed a plan and presented it to the company's leadership team. It was quickly adopted, and today, the insurance company is an industry leader in customer engagement—which has created a significant sales increase, particularly among younger customers.

Shannon's leadership in putting forward a vision for transforming her division from pushing communications out to pulling customers in—and building the brand through customer engagement—was very successful. It meets the following seven criteria of a successful vision statement, not unlike that of Henry Ford, President Kennedy, or Larry Page and Sergey Brin:

1. **The vision is simple and easy to understand.** Leaders must provide people with a clear picture of what the future will look like so that the team can readily understand the vision. Then contrast the vision with the current state. Shannon's vision of transforming her communications and branding division into a customer engagement model was clear, particularly when she enlisted the help of her staff in formulating it. When she pitched it to the leadership team, she was careful to build the business case for it by showing the return on investment (ROI) and what the department would look like after the transformation. Everyone got it very quickly.

2. **The vision is inspirational.** Not only do people understand it, but they love it, as well. It inspires them to believe that they are part of something new and exciting. I am sure that Shannon was able to get the vice president position because she demonstrated her passion for the idea. And, the division staff that Shannon talked to about the idea also was excited about it. Great visions get people excited and focused on a better future.

3. **The vision is a stretch.** You're not exactly sure how to implement it: You understand where you want to go, but all the pieces are not necessarily in place. You ask everyone to proceed on trust. But then again, everyone understands that the reward is worth the risk. I am sure President Kennedy had no clue how the United States was going to put a man on the moon in eight years, from the time he made the vision statement. Many things needed to be invented for that to happen. He just had confidence that the United States could be stretched to reach the very important goal of dominating the space race.

4. **The vision is transformative.** The vision proposes a significant change from the status quo. Notice that Shannon's goal of completely switching over the communications and branding division to a customer engagement strategy was absolutely transformative for that division. It took that staff in a whole new direction. The transformation probably required that Shannon rethink job titles, supplier relationships, internal communication strategies and a host of other changes in her division. A new vision should be transformative because it is all about reinventing.

5. **The vision is based on clear values.** What statement did Shannon make about the values of her insurance company, in setting a new vision? The most significant change was establishing a value for honoring customer voices concerning her company's products and services. The prior model did not really value customer input. Shannon's new approach placed that value front-and-center. A second value that Shannon changed was the need to listen to customers and to act on their ideas. Creating a value for acting on customer input was not only important for her division, but for the whole corporation. Everyone was going to have to do business differently in order to live up to the new approach she was creating.

6. **The vision is built on solid evidence.** It's important to contrast the future vision with the status quo. What evidence suggests that the status quo is not sustainable? "Why do we need to change?" a stakeholder might inquire. The case for change, as we know from Chapter 10, has to be clear. People needed to see the numbers to understand that the old way was choking the organization's ability to grow, since sales are so much less with unengaged customers. Sales were likely to triple when customer engagement moved past 70 percent, which was her two-year goal. She showed how many other companies had achieved similar growth.

7. **The vision is responsive to stakeholder needs.** Visions only really work when the stakeholders—the people responsible for implementing the vision—buy into the process. If President Kennedy had been the only person convinced we needed to win the space race, the vision would have fallen flat. In reality, this vision was a response to the Soviet Union (now Russia) being the first country to send a rocket into space. That was a real wake-up call for the nation, and the country demanded that the president do something about it. America was ready for a bold vision. Shannon's CEO, and ultimately her division, was also hungry for change.

## Step 2: Have simple goals

Having a conversation about vision usually scares people. They think that it's too daunting of a job, or simply over their heads. You'll see from the steps below, outlining how to win the Vision Game, that it begins by simply understanding stakeholders. A leader's job is to always and continuously understand stakeholders' needs and ambitions. This should be an ongoing effort in every department of every organization.

The point is that the Vision Game does not have to be done all at once, in a 30-minute meeting. It is probably a longer, critical conversation put together over time, with pieces that you may or may not already have in place.

To begin, think about any pieces of the vision that you already have in place. Pull them together and figure out what you need going forward. Keep the process focused and keep it simple. Take smaller steps to avoid unsettling people with too much change all at once. Vision conversations tend to energize people and can be a huge benefit to the work unit.

Before we talk about the stages of creating and implementing a vision, it would be useful to assess your own organization's vision.

## Vision Assessment Tool

Use these seven criteria to evaluate the vision of the organization you currently work for, or some other organization you are familiar with. The goal is to determine the extent to which this vision meets the criteria, and what could be done to improve the vision. Begin by stating the vision of the company or organization you wish to focus on, then examine the seven criteria. Score each with a 1 (criterion not met), 2 (criterion met partially), or 3 (criterion met completely).

Vision Statement: _____

_____

_____

| Criteria | Score 1, 2, 3 |
|---|---|
| 1.  It's simple and easy to understand | |
| 2.  It's inspirational | |
| 3.  It's a stretch | |
| 4.  It's transformative | |
| 5.  It's based on clear values | |
| 6.  It's built on solid evidence | |
| 7.  It's responsive to stakeholder needs | |

A score above 15 suggests that you have at least some aware-
ness of the effectiveness of the vision statement you focused on.
Sometimes, the easiest way to conduct this exercise is to focus
on the original vision of the organization you examined. When
an organization initially forms and prospers, it is generally in
response to a clear and compelling vision.

To continue to grow at an accelerated pace, an organization
needs to update its vision statement. The world changes. The
environment, the competition and the technology changes. So
do stakeholder needs and perceptions. The original vision may
be sorely outdated and in need of revision.

## Step 3: Select the right cards

Did you notice how many critical conversations about vision
that Shannon had in the course of implementing her vision? She
began her journey learning about customer engagement. Then
she had a conversation about it with her boss, the former vice
president, who rejected the idea. This conversation was followed
by an informal chat with the company CEO. Shannon then
interviewed for the vice president position and had more critical conversations about her vision. The conversations with staff
followed.

Every visioning stage involves a critical conversation that is
part of the Vision Game. The point is that taking the next step
in your organization generally involves playing the Vision Game.
As a result, the Leader Card should consist of topics and styles
that enable you to play it well, just like Shannon did.

Besides the Leader Card, what other cards are required to
play the Vision Game? Here are five cards that might be useful
for these important conversations:

1. **The Learner Card.** This is the first card a leader should
   play because it's important to first listen to stakeholders.
   What changes are needed to update or alter the current
   vision? What are people concerned and frustrated about?
   What are they excited about? What are their ambitions for
   themselves and for the organization? An effective leader

needs to understand what stakeholders are thinking and summarize that information, to ensure that the vision is responsive to these issues.

2. **The Colleague Card.** Shannon developed her original vision by listening to her colleagues about the organization and what could be done to improve it. She needed to demonstrate that she was part of the team and confirm they all wanted to move together in the new direction. That solidarity and cohesiveness is important in making sure the team will support the new direction.

3. **The Expert Card.** Forging a new direction requires leaning a great deal about what opportunities are out there and convincing others of the benefits of moving in a new direction. Leaders are expected to be knowledgeable about both the big-picture issues impacting the organization and the small details that are required to implement the new vision. Once a new vision has been created and presented to various audiences, the leader is in the business of proposing a significant change. Change creates uncertainty, and followers will be looking for the leader to reduce that uncertainty.

4. **The Friend Card.** A personal card is always needed in the course of these critical conversations. Talking to people as a friend reinforces your sensitivity to their personal situations and reinforces the fact that you understand that the new vision will impact them personally. Remember, people will always judge any change by how it impacts them personally, so make sure you are listening for those concerns.

5. **The Presenter Card.** The leader will be asked to give multiple presentations about the new vision. All aspects of becoming an expert presenter, described previously, apply here. Remember: Any vision needs to be sold over and over again, in various contexts. If you create the need for a new vision, then you are committing yourself to selling

it repeatedly. If you play your talk cards well, the Vision Game has a much greater chance of succeeding.

## Step 4: Play to win

Revising a company's vision (often called **reinvention**), or crafting a new vision, is conducted as a series of critical conversations of various forms. In total, these conversations form the Vision Game. These conversations should occur in a series of steps. Let's explore these steps and what they mean for you.

**Step 1: Identify stakeholders and participants.** Vision conversations ought to begin with stakeholders and participants. The trick is clearly identifying the real, active stakeholders and participants. Let's consider Shannon's insurance company, for example. Who is most affected by the implementation of Shannon's vision for turning the communications and branding division into a customer engagement model? Those directly involved might include:

- Executives and management
- Employees
- Customers
- Shareholders
- Employees' families

Those indirectly involved could include:

- Suppliers
- The local community
- Competitors
- The financial/insurance community
- Media

The purpose of identifying groups that are directly and indirectly effected by the change is to: a) involve some of these groups (certainly the most important ones) in creating and implementing the vision; b) learn the needs of each of these groups, to determine how to shape the vision; and c) create buy-in, because people are motivated by a vision that they can help create.

Perhaps the people inside the organization are the most important stakeholders. Senior leadership must be deeply involved and leading the process. After all, they have the power to sustain the switch and then wrap the whole organization around the switch. A customer engagement approach is not just a marketing change; it involves a whole different way of doing business. Without senior leadership being involved, the change will only limp along and create resentment.

**Step 2: Assess the future environment.** Once the stakeholders have been assembled, then the leader can begin playing the Driving-change Game, described in Chapter 7. Recall that the first step in playing this game is assessing the readiness for change. That requires looking into the future and determining if the organization's current direction will get it to where it needs to be in the future.

Shannon looked into the future to create her initial vision. How did she do that? She went to seminars and became educated about future trends in marketing and what other insurance companies were doing in marketing. She talked with colleagues in those other organizations to learn their experiences. She read trade publications that described how millennials are different than older generations and how they prefer different ways of communication and engagement.

Assessing the future environment should be comprehensive and systematic. It begins by asking a group of stakeholders to provide answers to a list of questions about the environment, including:

- What is the probable nature of future markets, customers and competition?
- What is the probable nature of the company's future business?
- What is the state of globalization of the company in the future?

- What are future technology changes, and how will these impact markets and the way services are purchased and provided?
- How will the company integrate information with suppliers and customers?
- What are likely future changes in employee skills?

Answers to these questions will provide a sense of whether the stars will align for a new vision. Shannon's answers to these questions pointed the way toward the need for a new customer engagement model.

Perhaps the most important question for Shannon to answer was the first one; after all, the market had changed. Younger customers expect more involvement with the companies they do business with. They expect to have input and to drive the brand. They also use technology differently and expect insurance services to be delivered faster and seamlessly. Once the stakeholders started considering these facts, it became clear that a change was needed for better corporate marketing.

**Step 3: Build the future vision.** By the time you're at Step 3 in the Vision Game, it may be clear that the old way of doing business is not sustainable, efficient or desirable. A change is needed—but to what? If steps 1 and 2 were implemented carefully, good options for future directions should emerge. In Shannon's case, she settled on a customer engagement vision for her division.

But Shannon probably considered other options, as well. Tweaking the "push" model of marketing might have been a good stop-gap model and wouldn't have ruffled too many feathers. In looking at the options available, it is important to consider the seven criteria from the beginning of this chapter that identify a high-quality vision.

Creating a new vision for an organization requires moving from generalities to specifics. To implement Shannon's vision of moving to a customer engagement model of marketing, what specifics would be needed? Here is a list of five questions that Shannon's plan might need to include:

1.  What is meant by "customer engagement"? How is it different than what is currently happening? What would be different for the customer?

2.  Who is setting the pace? What are other companies doing that is effective? What specific examples are available, and what kind of results have other companies had?

3.  How will we benchmark ourselves against the competition? Metrics are important here, in evaluating the change, to determine if it's effective. What three or four metrics are most important in judging effectiveness?

4.  What resources are needed to implement this model? Do we need different talent internally? Do we need different suppliers?

5.  What are the technology changes needed to make this work? What costs are associated with this kind of change?

Of course, there could be other questions, as well. Answering them is helpful in making a significant change attractive for stakeholders. New visions are often threatening to those invested in the status quo. Overcoming doubt, or open resistance, is best approached by thinking through the change very carefully.

# The Customer Engagement Game

While most of the critical conversations covered to this point are more management-related, this chapter focuses on critical conversations from a marketing perspective. This shift is important for leaders of every organization because customers' relationships with companies and organizations have changed. Customers want to engage with companies and build the company brand. Playing the Customer Engagement Game successfully requires a wide range of personal and professional cards, to ensure that customers feel welcomed and that their input is valued.

## What's a Brand?

Any company's brand, no matter how big or small, is vital to its health. A strong brand not only ensures strong sales growth, but it provides a hedge against company problems. In 2009, Toyota experienced a sudden acceleration problem with some of its large cars. Cars were, apparently, just rapidly accelerating despite driver attempts to control them.

*Customers want to engage with companies and build the company brand.*

The question is, what was to blame for this problem: Driver error or poor engineering by Toyota? If Toyota had a weak brand, meaning a reputation for poor quality and reliability, then customers (and the media) would probably want to blame Toyota. If Toyota had a history of cutting corners or cars breaking down, then the perception of Toyota having engineering problems would be easy for people to believe.

However, the Toyota brand, as a vehicle manufacturer, was so strong that most people blamed bad drivers for the problem. "Toyota would never let anything like this happen," many thought. The statement, "Their commitment to quality, safety and reliability are second to none" probably reflected most people's thinking. Even though Toyota had to pay $1.2 billion in fines for "hiding deadly unintended acceleration," the Toyota brand remains strong in the face of this crisis. The brand was simply too strong to be tarnished.

The same was not the case for Audi in the mid-1980s. They, too, had a sudden-acceleration problem, with cars allegedly taking off at will. Because Audi did not have a solid, established brand image associated with quality, safety and reliability, people were quick to blame the company—even though independent investigators were unable to find anything wrong with the crashed cars. Several years later, the company was actually absolved of any blame (drivers were at fault), but the damage had been done. Audi was blamed for the problem and sales plummeted. It took them many years to recover.

What these stories illustrate is the importance of a strong brand. In the broadest sense, a company's brand is its reputation, or image. If we dig deeper, we discover that the reputation is based on something that people value: a promise. In other words, a brand is really *a promise to deliver value.*

We have talked at length about value, so we know what that is. Customers engage companies to solve specific problems for them. Customers purchase products or services to satisfy their needs. The more satisfied they are that their needs have been met in relation to cost, the more value they derive from their purchases.

But, let's talk about a brand's promise. When someone makes a promise to do something in the future, e.g., pay back money, the other person must accept that promise. People accept promises if they believe that, in the future, the person will follow through. "I promise to pay you back," for example, is only accepted if the lender believes the person has a history of following through with his or her promises. Trust is the basis of promises accepted. It is a prediction about what will happen in the future.

This means that when a customer purchases a product or service and the company takes money for it, the customer accepts the company's promise that those products and services will do the job they're intended to do. The car will start and will perform exactly as expected. If customer expectations are met and exceeded on a routine basis, then trust emerges, promises are kept and the brand gets stronger.

Branding is not a new idea, of course. Companies have always been concerned about their reputations. What's new is that we now have the tools to rethink how brands are created and strengthened. The emergence of social media, and the mentality that feeds the popularity of social media, is new. Social media can blast a brand's promise, or its failure to deliver on its promise, around the globe. To understand this branding revolution let's first get a handle on the new consumer mentality called **customer engagement.**

## Step 1: Name the game

What's interesting about the Customer Engagement Game is that it's a critical conversation held in a multimedia context. Unlike most of the other games described in this book, which are primarily focused on face-to-face interactions, this game is much broader. Engagement happens through social media, face-to-face encounters and traditional media.

**What is customer engagement?** Customer engagement is all about bringing the customer inside your organization. To illustrate, consider Marcus, who is a millennial. He is 30 years old and a computer engineer for a large firm in Detroit. He is excited about working and living in downtown Detroit, which is becoming a hip place for millennials to live. Millennials love being in urban areas, where all the action is.

Since Marcus is a computer geek, he is very interested in the latest technology. He has developed many very specific and strongly held beliefs about how the technology he uses should perform. More importantly, he is not satisfied to simply sit back and wait for his preferred supplier, Dell, to send him whatever equipment and software they feel like sending. Marcus wants to interact with Dell and Dell users, to tell the company how its products and services should be configured.

Marcus even started a blog and a YouTube channel to connect with other Dell users and aficionados, to talk about the products and services. He updates his offerings weekly and has hundreds of followers. It's apparent that Dell is paying attention to Marcus's community, and to the other communities that are actively talking about its products and services. In fact, Dell regularly participates in these conversations and solicits feedback about new products and services.

The 2010s have brought a new relationship between companies and customers. No longer do customers expect to be passive recipients of marketing information and to have products pushed at them. Customers want to be engaged and directly connected to companies, and to help formulate the company's brand and products on a continual basis.

Instead of companies hiring intermediaries, like marketing firms, to cultivate the relationship between companies and customers, companies are linking directly with customers in real time to understand their needs and what brings value to their products and services. In fact, customers of multiple age groups expect direct access to companies. Social media provides this unprecedented access, and it has become the new normal.

This means your company or organization needs to rethink traditional marketing strategies. It is time to make the switch from marketing to customer engagement. It's time to shift from push marketing, where the goal is showering people with information, to pull marketing, where the goal is active engagement. It's a shift from using intermediaries to understand customers to interacting with them directly, to learn their needs and continuously adjust to them.

**Outside-in vs. inside-out companies.** From a broader perspective, companies that actively engage customers and pull them into their decision-making process are called "outside-in companies." These companies are customer-centric in all aspects of their products, services and business processes.

In contrast, "inside-out companies" take the view that company insiders know what's best for customers. These companies create products and services that are easiest and most convenient for them, regardless of customer input. Some of these inside-out companies believe that customers will just automatically buy their products and services. So why bother asking customers what's important to them?

It's easy to tell the difference between outside-in companies and inside-out companies. The former listen intently to customers and integrate them seamlessly into their company activities. The latter gather very little customer information, and if they do, it usually stays inside the marketing division and is rarely shared throughout the company. Which kind of company do you work in?

## Step 2: Have simple goals

"Pull marketing" means bringing customers into your organization as partners in creating and delivering your products and services. The goals of pulling customers into organizations are twofold:

1. **Affinity.** The first goal of any engagement strategy is to build affinity, or brand attractiveness. Especially millennials, but increasingly all age groups, want an emotional attachment to a brand and may begin to see it as an essential part of their lives. Marcus did that with Dell. He is very fond of Dell, as a brand, and identifies with it very strongly. Apple computer users often have the same affinity. They see themselves emotionally tied to all that Apple represents. When affinity is strong, people come back to the brand often, talk about it a great deal and influence others to get involved.

2. **Activity**. The second goal of engagement is to build activity or behavioral involvement. Companies want customers to blog about them, visit their websites, comment about their products and services and interact with other customers. If they have brick-and-mortar operations, then the goal is to also pull their customers into stores.

Are you ready to bring customers/members inside, to really understand them? Take the following Ten Touch Points for Brand Analysis Survey, to see how much you're in tune with customers, members or clients.

# Ten Touch Points for Brand Analysis

Below are listed 10 touch points, or areas in which your organization's brand is being presented to customers or members. These areas represent the sum total of the customer experience for your customers or members. To what extent do you understand their expectations at each of these touch points?

1. **Advertising:** The first touch point for most companies is information outreach, which generally takes the form of advertising. The message must continuously focus on the brand and the value it brings to the customer. Are these outreach attempts targeted to specific markets, and multimedia-oriented to ensure media saturation?

2. **Marketing:** Marketing efforts to touch customers generally focus on different strategies that go beyond advertising to expose the products and services to the target audiences. These might include trade shows, special events, celebrity endorsements, press releases and the like.

3. **Sales:** Many organizations have a sales staff that reaches out to specific customer groups. The online sales experience is also included in this category. Is the sales process consistent with the brand identity?

4. **In-store/on-site experience:** Hopefully the advertising, marketing and sales efforts can attract people to the place where the products and services are offered, including the online venue. What do potential customers experience when they enter this space, given the value proposition the brand is trying to promote?

5. **Ordering/purchasing/buying:** When customers select products to purchase, they have to pay in some manner. Is the ordering/purchasing/buying experience consistent with the brand's identity?

6. **Delivery:** If customers don't immediately acquire their products or services after purchase, what is their delivery experience? Delivery might include follow-up surveys

about services purchased or notifications about changes. Does this service meet or exceed customer expectations?

7. **Installation:** After delivery, some products or services require professional installation. This might include adding software or getting a system up and running in its final location. Does this touch point enable customers to use the product or service as intended and to full potential?

8. **Product performance:** Perhaps the most critical touch point is the actual use of the product or service. Does the customer use the product or service frequently and find that it solves the problem in a reliable and consistent fashion?

9. **Support:** Many times, customers have questions or problems. Can they easily contact knowledgeable resources? Are these inquiries handled in a manner consistent with the brand?

10. **Engagement:** Finally, after the customer has had interaction with the products and services, how is the organization bringing these individuals inside the company, to listen to them? Is there a virtual strategy using social media? Is there a physical strategy, in which individuals are assisted in some way or linked into networks of others who use the products and services?

## The Customer Experience Assessment

Below, indicate the extent to which you believe that your company collects data (of any kind) to learn about customers' experiences for each of these 10 touch points. On a scale of 0-10, with 0 representing no data collected and 10 being extensive data collected, rate your company:

| Customer/Member Touchpoints | Score 0-10 |
|---|---|
| 1.  Advertising | |
| 2.  Marketing | |
| 3.  Sales | |
| 4.  In-store/on-site experience | |
| 5.  Ordering/purchasing/buying | |
| 6.  Delivery | |
| 7.  Installation (process and placement) | |
| 8.  Product performance | |
| 9.  Support | |
| 10. Engagement | |
| **Total Score:** | |

If you scored below 50, you believe that your organization may not be tuned in to customer expectations at each of these touch points. A score below 50 suggests that gathering these data is not a priority, which may give you the label of being an "inside-out company." If your score is between 50 and 70, then you are probably working to be more responsive to customers. If your score is over 70, then you believe that you are fairly effective in learning about customer expectations, thereby giving you the label of an "outside-in company."

## Step 3: Select the right cards (for customer engagement)

Customers expect to interact with companies. Customers want companies to play a variety of cards in these conversations. Here is the minimum set of cards that a company should be playing in the Customer Engagement Game:

1. **The Learner Card.** This card is important because companies today must adopt the position that they want to learn from their customers. What's important

to customers? What value do they derive from your company's products and services? How do they use them in the course of their lives?

The auto industry knows that customers don't just want transportation. To satisfy their identity and entertainment needs, customers want vehicles that are not only reliable but also stylish and sexy. Many people view cars as an extension of themselves, and not just as transportation. Yet this view might change with each generation of buyers, and car companies will have to relearn market preferences. The key is constantly learning from customer engagement.

1. **The Friend Card.** To build affinity and energy, companies must occasionally play the Friend Card with customers. This move encourages customers to reciprocate with the Friend Card, so the company and the customers get to know one another. The more the company can be seen as having a human face, the more customers will become attached to it.

   For example, a highly successful credit union that boasts many college student members actively engages these students with programs that go beyond financial literacy. The credit union asks students to create and implement a broad range of programs and activities important for student success. It engages these students with the Friend Card by providing many kinds of personal and career advice in the course of these interactions. This engagement has created a great deal of brand affinity for the credit union among students.

1. **The Expert Card.** Customers also want and expect that companies will be experts in their areas. People working on the front line with customers, including phone staff and greeters, should be able to talk knowledgeably about the industry, their own products and services, and maybe even the competition. People are more information-hungry in an age when Google and others have put a

world of information at everyone's fingertips. We expect that company representatives can go beyond what we can get on Google and make us feel like an insider.

2. **The Entertainer Card.** Branding is all about the heart, not just the brain. Remember, affinity is an emotional condition—the desire to be part of the brand and share the experience. Successful companies always want to make people feel a certain way when interfacing with their brands. Often, the Entertainer Card does that. It makes the company seem fun, engaged—perhaps even irreverent. Many people, particularly millennials, want to be a part of something fun and edgy.

## Step 4: Play to win: critical conversations and customer engagement

If you want to be an outside-in company that builds brand affinity and activity, what needs to happen? First, at each touch point, your company must start pulling customers inside your organization. Second, individuals at all levels of the organization must listen to, and more importantly, respond to, what customers have to say. And third, the culture of the organization must be reinvented to be customer-centric. Let's break down each of the requirements for becoming an outside-in company.

**Pulling customers inside.** The line between customers and employees in the more progressive companies is blurring. For example, virtually all auto manufacturers now use online communities to advise them on methods of improving each of the 10 touch points identified previously. Participants in these communities are typically individuals who want to provide feedback about their experiences. But they are also people who want to interact with one another. The companies that create and manage the online communities for companies have proprietary social media sites that enable community members to talk with one another and with company representatives. They share videos, pictures and stories to better understand one another and communicate.

These are critical conversations that require a wide variety of talk cards, as we've just learned. Company members sharing insights with customers, either at live clinics or in a social media exchange, might play the Expert Card (talking about technical issues), the Friend Card (sharing family stories) or the Leader Card (asking questions and summarizing interactions).

**Listening at all levels.** The question is, who is having these critical conversations? Is it just the marketing staff or the customer service representatives? The 10 touch points listed above indicate that customers interact with many parts of an organization. All of these staff members help to build and maintain the brand—not just marketing or customer service members.

In my work with companies, I insist on exposing workshop participants to customer/member input. Since customer contact is often very limited in larger companies, the customer input is generally very eye-opening. I recall one group of participants I took to a customer focus panel. At first, the company participants were reluctant to speak up. However, when the customers started talking about touch points that were directly related to the participants' respective units, they had lots of questions. A rich dialogue took place, including the identification of specific bottlenecks and points of customer irritation.

The point is that in many companies, only a few front-line people are specifically tasked with listening to customers—and they are often not sought out by decision-makers and higher-ups in the organization because they're phone or window workers. It's easier to be an inside-out company, but it's harder to stay in business that way, not connected to customer feedback. In contrast, it's harder to be an outside-in company and actually listen to customers, but you're more likely to stay in business that way.

**Reinventing the culture.** If the company's culture resists or outright refuses to let customers inside, then doing things like gathering data on touch points or allowing people at all levels to listen to customers becomes very difficult. What are the key cultural elements that must be addressed in order to become more customer-centric? Think of culture as a set of values. What does the company value? Here are eight cultural values that every outside-in company should have:

1. **Management buy-in.** People in upper management need to clearly and consistently embrace the "customer revolution" approach to engagement. The message needs to be simple and frequently stated.

2. **Innovation talk.** Employees must have dedicated time to process customer feedback and reflect on how it might change the company's products, services and/or internal systems. Many companies form dedicated groups or off-site teams that take on significant barriers to building customer value.

3. **Competition scope.** Companies must commit to discovering what competitors are doing that promotes engagement. What kind of business success are they having? What professional associations help understand industry trends in customer engagement—and how should your employees get involved?

4. **Customer stories.** Every customer has a story about using the products and services that your company promotes. The stories provide vivid detail about the value of your products and services to the customer. It's vital that you capture these stories and showcase them throughout the company in order to help employees better understand customers.

5. **Flattened management.** Decision-making in a customer-centric company must be swift and efficient. That requires an organization that does not have endless layers of management. What can you do to streamline your company's decision-making in order to respond more quickly to customer feedback?

6. **Inter-unit engagement.** Not only must customer feedback filter through the company, but disparate units in the company must be brought together to address issues that customers raise. The fewer silos, the better. If your company is full of silos, then horizontal linkages must be built in order to form customer-centric teams. How often are you involved in inter-departmental meetings? Is the agenda interactive, so people can brainstorm ideas to address customer issues?

7. **Risk-taking.** Building customer value in products and services requires risk-taking. Upper management needs to make it clear that risks are an essential part of the company's growth and will be rewarded.

8. **Risk rewarding.** Speaking of rewarding risk, the final piece of the customer-centric culture pie is all about risk: being specific and clear about what risk means, how employees are expected to take risks and how risk will be factored into performance appraisals. If these elements are not clear, then no one will take a risk.

# Customer Engagement Case Study: Amazon

In a recent blog post, Pauline Ashenden, an authority on customer experience, identified five customer experience innovations that keep Amazon moving forward in both revenue and profitability. These five illustrate the importance of gaining customer perspectives on what's required in order to maximize the customer experience:

1. **Make it simple.** Amazon innovated One-click Shopping and offers the option of ordering through Twitter, in efforts to keep checkout sales quick and easy. Customer service takes the same approach by making it easy to return items.

2. **Share the experience.** Amazon was the first company to have customer reviews, which is an excellent engagement strategy. These reviews are common now, and are widely viewed by consumers as very credible.

3. **Offer what customers want.** Brick-and-mortar stores limit what customers can buy, but Amazon has much fewer restrictions. Amazon software allows the company to personalize offers and recommendations based on a customer's previous purchase history. They listen to the customer and engage with their interests.

4. **Keep innovating.** Amazon started as an online bookstore. The brand then grew, using that experience as a pattern to build customer trust that could be leveraged as a great place to shop. Amazon never focused on internal talents when deciding whether or not to expand. They looked at customer need, like having a Kindle e-reader for the electronic books, and *then* acquired the internal expertise they needed in order to satisfy demand. Constant innovation is a core part of the climate.

5. **Always put customers first.** Competitors are not first at Amazon. The philosophy has been focused on putting customers first, because if that's done well, there's no need to worry about the competition. They took a long-term view in building the business, knowing how important it is to build brand affinity and activity, so they could serve customers for a long time.

# Avoiding Common Mistakes

Critical conversations are stressful, and sometimes, they are spontaneous as well. When people are unprepared to perform well during critical conversations, they may try to avoid them or stumble through them. At this point, you should feel fairly well-equipped to have the critical conversations covered in previous chapters.

Yes, mistakes will happen. Even the most seasoned veterans of critical conversations can slip into bad habits or move the conversation in an unproductive direction. The key in minimizing such slip-ups is being aware of the most common mistakes that can happen during tense interactions.

## Mistake 1: Playing only one card

Do you remember Philip from Chapter 1? He could only play the Salesperson Card in just about every situation. When he tried to talk with his daughter, he failed—and it was because he had used the Salesperson Card. He did not display the Parent Card, which has very different topics and styles.

The explanation provided in Chapter 1 focused on the idea of **trained incapacity**. What capacitates someone to be an effective communicator in one situation completely incapacitates him or her in a different situation. With Philip's Salesperson Card, he tends to view people first as a customer, rather than as a spouse or friend.

Donna is a physician. She decided to become a pediatrician, since she loves helping children. She is very talented and works hard, seeing many patients each day in a very busy practice. I was working with her on a project when we had several conversations about a variety of personal and professional issues.

In each conversation, I felt like she was talking to me as a patient, while playing the Doctor Card. She seldom revealed much personal information, but (like a good physician) wanted to know everything about me. Her style was friendly, but not too friendly. Her language and styles choices were also formal and with some amount of power, as she made suggestions about what to do.

What Philip and Donna have in common is the bad habit of trained incapacity. They have difficulty playing more than the one card they use at work all the time. Do you have that same challenge? Playing only one card makes it tough to be truly effective in critical conversations. As you have learned, critical conversations require several cards, along with the ability to switch cards with ease.

It's important to point out that relying on one card also restricts style choices. When Philip plays the Salesperson Card, his style choices are generally very friendly, informal and high-power. When those style choices are inappropriate, he has a hard time adjusting. Again, one card and one set of style choices is very limiting.

My recommendation is to first be reflective about the cards you are playing at all times. Do you see variety? Do your friends see variety? Can you switch topics and styles that reflect these different card choices? Second, place yourself in a variety of situations that allow you to practice playing different cards. This practice should help break the habit of over-reliance on one card and the problem of trained incapacity.

## Mistake 2: Playing the wrong card

A second mistake that often hampers communicators is playing the wrong card at the wrong time. This error can happen for one of two reasons. The most common reason people play the wrong card is that they misread the situation, so they unintentionally play the wrong card.

One of my workshop participants, Alex, told me how playing the wrong card at a social engagement caused him some grief. Alex is an American who travels internationally a great deal. Once, on a business trip to Japan, he attended a very formal social event hosted by a prominent Japanese client. His boss was present, so the expectation by the Japanese was that Alex's boss would do most of the talking. Alex forgot that Japan is a country in which hierarchy matters a great deal: underlings are expected to talk less than the leader. When asked a question at dinner, Alex played the Expert Card and went on too long with his detailed answer, which prevented his boss from demonstrating his own expertise. Later, one of the hosts was overheard wondering if Alex's boss was a qualified leader.

Certainly Alex did not intentionally undermine his boss by playing the Expert Card. If he more fully understood Japanese culture, he would have deferred to his boss and played the Employee Card.

On the other hand, sometimes people try to play the Comedian Card and fall flat, because either the humor is not funny or it's inappropriate for the situation. The key is to be very thoughtful about card choice, given the situation.

A second common reason a person plays the wrong card is that he or she does not listen, as it is through listening that someone determines the card the other communicator is asking him or her to play. Philip had this problem with is daughter. When his daughter approached him with a personal challenge, she was tacitly asking him to play the Parent Card. Since Philip was not comfortable playing the Parent Card, he played the Salesperson Card instead, with unfortunate consequences.

This is a common problem. People often don't listen carefully to one another to determine what card the others are asking them to play. When the issues are personal, people generally want the other to play cards from their personal deck. When the issues are professional, pulling from the professional deck is most appropriate. Most people don't specifically signal which card they want the other to play; it just has to be figured out.

Avoiding the problem of playing the wrong card at the wrong time involves both attention paid to the situation and careful listening. Being thoughtful about these issues will generally result in playing the right card at the right time.

## Mistake 3: Allowing your communication style to block sound card choices

In Chapter 3, you assessed your own communication style. If your scores on the content- or topic-focused part of the scale were much higher than the relation-focused portion, you may have trouble listening to and managing relationship messages. If you are primarily content-focused, you are less likely to be tuned in to the other communicator's style choices—which are usually good hints at determining the cards that person wants you to play.

A friend recently told me a story about having trouble connecting with his wife. After a few minutes of conversation, I learned that when his wife starts talking to him using sad, unhappy, informal and low-power styles, he doesn't realize that she's asking him to play the Husband Card, and listen to her concerns. He doesn't hear those style-choice messages. He probably would have low relationship scores in the Communication Style Inventory, from Chapter 3. This tendency restricts his ability to pay attention to his wife's card-choice style changes, which signal relationship and connection needs. He should make a conscious effort to emphasize the Husband Card, and thereby increase his ability to connect with his wife on many levels.

On the other hand, consider someone whose style is more relationship-focused. That person is at risk for overlooking important content components of the message. People with low interest in being precise or in developing a topic thoroughly are likely to pass over these considerations, which may cause them to avoid hard topics that require detailed attention. This lack of topical discipline might prevent these individuals from playing the Expert Card or the Leader Card, when needed.

Social leaders in groups often display a communication style that is heavy on relationship cues and light on content information. They want everyone to feel involved, happy and valued. That's important, but don't ask these individuals to play the Expert Card—the one that requires them to dig deep into the subject matter—because that's not their priority. Their style limits their card options.

## Mistake 4: Playing the wrong game

As we know from previous chapters, when people start playing a Card Talk game, they are essentially asking others to play along with that game. The annual holiday lunch with my colleagues is a purely social event, meant to celebrate another successful year in the trenches. Each of us tells funny family holiday shopping experiences. Each story reinforces the importance of playing the Personal Story-sharing Game, and makes it less and less appropriate to play more serious, work-related games.

Picking up a concept from the Communication Games Triangle in Chapter 5, the holiday lunch is a casual conversation situation that really does not call for moving interaction into the problem-solving zone. No one wants to talk about any important, work-related issue, nor play a decision-making game of any sort.

My colleague's son has mild autism. A key characteristic of individuals with mild autism is the inability to read social cues and know how to respond appropriately to others in a social setting. For such individuals, playing the Teasing Game may be difficult, because he or she isn't likely to pick up on the teasing intent. The person is more likely to view it as the Criticism Game, rather than as a game aimed at building relational bonds. With people who are not equipped to interpret games, the nature of the game has to be very clear, so that the talk card can be reciprocated appropriately.

Listening comes into play here. Can you listen closely in order to determine what game others are asking you to play? This is often difficult in a crowd of people who all know one another well, when you are the new person. They are all used to playing very subtle, personal games, and you may not under-stand what's going on. Over time, you might pick it up, but you might not realize they are teasing one another, for example.

## Mistake 5: Bringing up the wrong topic

A fifth mistake that many people make involves bringing up a topic that is inconsistent with the card being played, or is inap-propriate for the situation. I attended an academic talk several years ago by a noted professor. As the talk began, the professor started going over material that everyone in the audience already knew and that was several years out of date. We were all amazed that he didn't talk about his new research, which we thought was the purpose of the talk.

In short, the professor picked the wrong topic for his highly informed audience. This is quite common. A speaker trying to play the Expert Card misreads an audience and picks a topic that is either too elementary or too complicated. When this mis-take happens, the audience quickly stops listening. The lesson to be learned is that conducting an audience analysis before speak-ing is necessary in order to pick just the right topics that the audience expects or needs to hear.

This same mistake happens when people misread the commu-nication context and pick a topic that is inappropriate for that situation. Have you ever had a conversation in which both of you were playing the Friend Card, and one of you brought up a topic that was really out of line? Maybe it was too personal. Or maybe it involved the Teasing Game, and the other person was just not in the mood to be teased at that particular point in time.

Avoiding inappropriate topic or game choices involves better reading of your audience. What do they expect? What might impress them? What cards and style choices will work best? Reading the audience is the first step in winning critical conversations. Don't shortcut this process!

## Mistake 6: Making weak style choices

Dana was an attendee at one of my workshops focusing on giving effective PowerPoint presentations. Dana was asked by her boss to attend because she had received some negative feedback about the quality of her presentations. It's not that her ideas were bad, but her presentations lacked passion and intensity. It looked like she was just trying to get through them, with little regard for whether the audience understood what she was talking about. Dana's style was not friendly. It was also very formal and demonstrated very low power.

After attending the workshop, Dana reported in an email that she had received some very positive feedback about her new presentation style. She reported that she was now showing more enthusiasm, playing more diverse talk cards during her presentation, moving around the room and speaking more confidently.

Alexis had this same problem when playing the Performance Appraisal Game. Recall that at the beginning of performance appraisals, the goal is to have a friendly, informal general conversation about what's happening with the employee. But Alexis was unable or unwilling to communicate using these styles. She was not friendly, too formal and too high-power during this initial phase of performance appraisals. These style choices turned off the employee's willingness to openly share information that would be important to explore.

Alexis could fix this mistake by being aware of her bad style choices. Maybe no one has ever pointed out that her style choices send the wrong message to the other communicators. My guess is that Alexis, and others with the same problem as

Alexis, make these choices out of habit and do not act this way on purpose.

The second fix for this mistake is to make an effort to better prepare for these situations. Alexis needed to decide what style choices to use and then practice using them more often, to overcome the problem of trained incapacity.

## Mistake 7: Rushing through the conversation

I hate to pick on our star salesman Philip, the guy who had trouble playing something other than the Salesperson Card when communicating with his daughter, yet his case is a classic illustration of the "rushing" mistake. Recall that his high-pressure job required him to deal with individual sales problems quickly and decisively. He approached every conversation with this same mentality—he was in a big hurry!

**First, slow down and understand.** In any given critical conversation, take time to first read what cards the other is playing and understand what cards you're being asked to play. Philip failed to do this with his daughter and it cost him. His daughter was asking him to play the Parent Card and he didn't understand that, because he was intent on hastening the conversation.

The point is that you should not attempt to speed up critical conversations by assuming that people are going to play the same cards all the time. In the Performance Appraisal Game, an employee might begin with the Friend Card rather than the Employee Card. Listen first and be prepared for that. In the Negotiation Game, the other person might play the Dictator Card and try to intimidate you into submission. Listen, and then be prepared for that.

Once you develop a good understanding of what games people are playing and what cards they are using to play that game, you can adjust and figure out how to respond. Failing to listen and understand creates all kinds of problems in critical conversations. Listen, and don't rush!

**Second, stay calm.** I have taught courses in sales communication for which students go through many different role-playing exercises. In one such session, I asked a professional salesperson to play the role of a client; a student played the role of the salesperson, trying to get the client to sign up for a subscription. The first thing the professional client did, at my request, was to tell the student-salesperson that the price for the subscription was too high. When dealing with price objections, I tell students not to negotiate on price right away, but to take the time to understand why the client feels that way.

Predictably, the student salesperson panicked and did not seek to understand, but rather immediately lowered the price. Of course, the client continued to indicate that the price was too high, and the student kept lowering the price—basically begging the client to sign up for the subscription! At that point I stopped the role play. Upon reflection, the student admitted that he had panicked and had not taken the time to probe the client's objection.

Critical conversations often cause people to panic. The Communication Games Triangle explains why. When we move from the Casual Conversation Game to the Problem-solving Game, and further into the Conflict Game, our identities are on the line. When we switch from the Friend Card to a professional card of some kind, or a more difficult personal card, people expect us to perform well using that card. Those expectations put our identities on the line. We're being judged! Sometimes, when we know we're being judged, we panic. We just want to get through the critical conversation to avoid being judged.

The more you practice playing the Leader Card, for example, the more confident you will become about playing those more demanding professional and personal cards. You will know when they're needed, what topics to use when playing them, what styles are appropriate and how to win games when playing them. Confidence is key. Practice, take your time and don't panic. It's a winning formula for successful critical conversations!

# Final Thoughts

I wrote this book because critical conversations are such a defining feature of effective leadership. Playing the Leader Card means that others expect the individual to perform effectively in all talk card games. I have talked with many leaders who doubt their ability to play many of the games discussed in this book. Granted, some of the games are very difficult to play effectively. Yet leaders will have a difficult time making progress without learning how to do them well.

The real challenge is simply jumping in and making the most of the opportunity. My goal is to provide you with tips on how to perform well in these diverse contexts. Review these often, to keep you on the path to effective game performance. I wish you well!

*Bill Donohue, 2018*

CPSIA information can be obtained
at www.ICGtesting.com
Printed in the USA
LVHW101315010922
727306LV00004B/491

9 781641 800082